T0288070

Zero Point Poiesis

Zero Point Poiesis

George Quasha's Axial Art

Edited, with an Introduction
Burt Kimmelman

Foreword
Jerome McGann

AporeiA
NEW YORK

Copyright © 2022 Burt Kimmelman. All rights revert to individual authors upon publication.

All rights reserved.

11 12 13 7 6 5 4 3 2 1 First Edition

Aporeia, is an imprint of Marsh Hawk Press, Inc.

Except for short passages for purpose of review, no part of this book may be reproduced in any form or by any means, electronic or mechanical, including printing, photocopying, recording, or by any information storage or retrieval system, without permission in writing from the author(s) and the Publishers.

Design: Susan Quasha
Cover art detail: George Quasha, Axial drawing

ISBN: 978-0-9986582-2-3

Library of Congress Cataloging-in-Publication Data Available

Axial poiesis works to reveal language at zero point—
the open and undefinable matrix where its potential
for further life remains unlimited.

George Quasha

Waking from Myself (preverbs)

Axial Drawing (graphite & color pencil, two-handed), 2008

Contents

Jerome McGann

Foreword

When I first discovered George Quasha's *preverb* volumes five years ago, which for a while became my regular nighttime reading, my immediate experience was a thrilled (=physical) glimpse of the presence of an "implicate order." Preverbs are not "poems" but poetic music that keeps extruding itself out of itself because all the words are feeding off a kind of Pythagorean reservoir of language that has been lived and is still living and breathing. And it isn't the glimpse of the "order" that's so affecting. It's the energy shock that drives in and through the local language moment/space/object.

The preverbial genre, and it is a kind of genre, has been fashioned from the morphogenetic music of Blake, whose "Proverbs of Hell" are its manifest source and end and test; and as with Blake, the music moves to open doors of perception through the chief inlets of soul in this age, the senses. Who knew that so many doors had been locked shut in our prison-housed language? Perhaps we all knew it but just kept forgetting. That must be what Edward Lear meant to remind us of when he wrote: "We think so then and we thought so still."

Quasha's preverbial music reminds me that many ears have heard this music. I think of G. Spencer Brown's meta-mathematical *Laws of Form* and of the Blessed Raymon Llull's combinatoric masterpiece the *Ars Magna*, of Alfred Jarry's *Exploits and Opinions of Doctor Faustroll, 'Pataphysician* and of Randall McLeod's close empirical studies of Obliterature. But most of all I remember Llull's twentieth-century inheritor, Raymond Queneau and his elementary hornbook *Foundations of Literature*.[1]

---

[1] I give here convenient reference editions. Reading or unreading Blake has been made more widely available by the great online (freely available) *William Blake Archive*. See also G. Spencer Brown, *Laws of Form* (London: Allen and Unwin, 1969); Raymon Llull, *Ars Magna* (1305) in *Selected Works of Ramon Llull*, trans. Anthony Bonner, 2 vols. (Princeton UP: Princeton, 1985); Alfred Jarry, *Exploits and Opinions of Doctor Faustroll, 'Pataphysician: a neo-scientific novel*, translated

For my purposes, the key passage in Queneau comes as theorem 3 and its natural consequent theorem 7, both of which he derives from the third of the second group of his foundational axioms, the so-called "Axioms of Order." According to theorem 3, "Where two words are present, the sentence in which they appear includes at least one word between these two words." Consequently, theorem 7: "Between two words of a sentence there exists an infinity of other words." Anticipating the "surprise" that these two theorems can occasion, Queneau adds the following comment: "To overcome his astonishment and understand these theorems [the reader] need only admit the existence of what we shall call … 'imaginary words' and 'infinitesimal words'. Every sentence contains an infinity of words; only an extremely limited number of them is perceptible; the rest are infinitesimal or imaginary."

Of course one cannot *see* those imaginary words—at least *I* can't. Perhaps Pythagoras, perhaps even Plato, could. Whatever, because the sounds they code can be heard (made) and their rhythms felt (performed), the "imaginary" words might be reborn in the mind's ears. So an ideal light sings from the shadows that light made possible, flooding our world with its infinitesimal words.

Reading any of Quasha's preverbial sequences makes me aware that he has trained his body to a regular attentiveness to those unheard melodies. Sometimes I am struck at some particular moment or line—*Mein Gott*, he's done it again—but then it keeps happening and I find myself more struck by a pervasive discipline by which his "me" disappears. And so the light of sense goes out with a flash, and an invisible world appears. What is remarkable is how these metamorphoses play out semantically

& annotated by Simon Watson Taylor, Introduction by Roger Shattuck (Exact Change: Boston, MA, 1996); Raymond Queneau, *The Foundations of Literature (After David Hilbert)*, in *Oulipo Laboratory*, trans. Harry Mathews and Iain White (Atlas Press: London, 1995). Although Randall McLeod's work on Obliterature has been a lifelong endeavor, the key essay is "Obliterature: *Reading a Censored Text of Donne's 'To his mistres going to bed',*" *English Manuscript Studies* 12 (2005); see also "*THE UNEDITOR: Randall McLeod in conversation with Mark Owens, July 2008,*" in *Dot Dot Dot* 18 (24 August 2009): 40–57.

("There's no wiggle room without a body"—Quasha) as well as syntactically—though I judge that the path of syntax is Quasha's preferred path. But being preferred, it makes those semantic/metaphoric moments still more startling when they come, as when a preverb plays off a proverb: "No time is like the present." Such a tiny transcendence, a grain of grand!

Quasha's style with this Blakean sense of language, dominantly inflected by Whitman, is focused on what Wagner called "the music of the future." So his preverbs are regularly "pre" oriented. The voices they hear and speak seem to want to run over the horizons of the ends of the lines—stopped somewhere waiting for you/me/us. Swinburne is a nice and interesting contrast, for the voices he hears and summons out of his language are definitely located at the sentence's other horizon line—the space before the sentence ever began, in the other eternity that Shelley called "the dark backward and abysm of time," especially from the time before the gods were driven from the world. "Do you hear this, Amphiarus, in your home beneath the earth?" Shelley quoted/asked that question, and Swinburne reprised it. For Swinburne, memory IS the mother of the muses, and the music of the future—see the great conclusion to "Anactoria"—is a gift of love to the "mother and lover of men."

How deeply Romantic are Quasha's commitments. I mean "Romantic" in the sense drawn out in, say, "Auguries of Innocence"—as opposed, for instance, to the dark apocalypses in *Europe* or "The Book of Urizen" (the Lambeth books in general). The rubric for such a stance is "A thing of beauty is a joy for ever"—a statement which, however, is as false as it is true, and for us now MORE false because it is proposed as true in Keats's presentation. So when Charles Bernstein rewrites it "A thing of beauty should annoy for ever," the truth of Keats' "error" gets reborn by showing how ANNOYING the line can seem and feel to an attentive spirit. *Duendes* are not necessarily friendly, are they, nor should they be.

Reading the most recent volume of preverbs, *Not Even Rabbits Go Down This Hole*, I am constantly brought up short, breathtaken ("halted without an effort to break through"). It happened right away, with the first section of "The First House." Swinburne aspired, he once wrote, to become "now no more a singer, but a song," and he often managed to do just that—as another great poet once wrote, "And thus I am absorbed, and this is life." Such words and passages kept singing through my mind as I read this wonderful book, and I mention the first of his preverbings in this context because the music of this writing is so completely realized, as if his song could have no ending. Wordsworth wanted to "see into the life of things." Jeffrey Herrick, a poet of Quasha's ilk, has called that the life of sings.

I could quote a long list of passages, individual lines, that just bouleversed me—they strike like certain moments in music that leave you feeling there's nothing more to say AND THEN, in and from that feeling, a wonderment explodes because you realize at exactly the same moment, which is fleeing on, that "there is no end in sight." I keep quoting poetry that runs through my head and heart because the proper commentary on such work is not "explication" of meaning, which we use for poetry committed to "poems," but just more poetry, more music.

How deeply apt that term "preverb" is. "Poems," especially when they're approached with meaning-making interpretive moves, are in mortal danger of being read and judged for their wisdom ("proverbial"). As Poe understood so well, that hunger for meaning is a fearful temptation, signaling as it does an urge to take flight from experience to didactic comforts. But as in music, poetry's rests work best when they are tense and arresting. So is poetry's desire, as the poet said, for "rest, but not to feel 'tis rest." "Comforter, where is thy comforting" another poet once asked, and the answer was already right there, arisen in the music of those five echoing words.

"Language *is* music" Harry Partch once truly said. All poets know this and some, like George Quasha, want to take it not so much as their subject as their very instrument. "Make me thy lyre, even as the forest is." Thinking that way, as Quasha does too, enlists poetry in an important adventure: a daring quest to play instruments that a world of getting and spending keeps trying to turn instrumental. Those are services language can perform but they turn to killing labors if we don't keep Quasha's sure sense that the ways of the world of language are the ways of singing birds.

So just consider the lilies of his field.

Burt Kimmelman

Introduction

This book assembles sixteen critical appreciations of George Quasha's singular achievement in the arts, plus an interview with him on his poetics. His presence in the life and work of a great many poets, painters, sculptors, musicians and media artists has been remarkable. The book contains a range of assessments, mainly of his original poetic genre, the *preverb,* and its core focus, the "axial principle," as well as how the latter applies to other *axialities,* which go by names like "axial stones," "axial drawing," and "axial music." Axiality, as he sees it, goes beyond the art context to a core *life* principle.

Written by luminaries in their own right, these assessments are meant to broaden awareness of Quasha's extraordinary artistic accomplishments together with the thinking that lies behind them—a body of thought that constitutes a major contribution to poetics. The evolution of such thinking has been deeply entwined with the events of his life and the people with whom he has worked over the years. It seems well worth bringing a brief account of all this history to the fore.

Quasha was born in White Plains, New York in 1942. He and his older brother Robert were raised by a single mother who moved to Miami, Florida when they were young. A musician at fourteen, he was a drummer in his high school band when it performed in Havana, Cuba for the famous annual parade band members looked forward to. He was reading Thoreau and Eliot then, but it was Nietzsche's writings that quickly brought him to a definitive break with conventional religion. Indeed, it led to a life-long mistrust of institutions; and this would be a factor shaping his entire life.

He won the Florida State debate championship at fifteen. One of his debate opponents, another state champion, was Gary Shapiro, who is now a philosopher and Nietzsche scholar, as well as art historian (and a contributor to this book). George attended the University of Miami, the summer after high school, and debated in the national debate tournament there. It was in this context that, at sixteen, he won a scholarship to the newly founded and idiosyncratic International School of America, a project of Ohio educator Karl Jaeger, a month later joining a dozen or so high school graduates from around the country (Dr. Andrew Weil among them).

They flew around the world for the next nine months, accompanied by a sizable cohort of university faculty, living mostly with local families in some thirteen countries from Asia and the Middle East to Europe. They read locally focused books, visited factories, farms, and museums, and regularly attended classes. A photo-essay on the school appeared in *Life Magazine*, when they'd visited archeological sites in Egypt; several of the pictures were taken by Quasha in his role as school photographer.

One of the teachers was the political journalist and China specialist Edgar Snow (who became Quasha's mentor). Another was the Ohio artist Emerson Burkhart, who proved to be an enthusiastic guide through each country's museums. Snow's international cachet gave the students entrée to the likes of Eleanor Roosevelt, I.F. Stone, Jawaharlal Nehru, Rajendra Prasad, and Willie Brandt. (Snow is credited with, a decade later, helping arrange the Nixon visit to China.)

After a year of being intensely on the move, Quasha spent the summer in Paris, learning French and "pretty much living in the Louvre." He then attended Ohio State University where he studied poetry with Milton Kessler, German with Sigurd Burckhardt, and philosophy with Morris Weitz, three teachers who lad a lasting impact on him. Still mentally in travel mode, however, and impatient with Columbus, Quasha leapt at the chance to spend the winter quarter at Mexico City College, where he studied Spanish, anthropology, and geology. The following year at OSU served mainly as prelude to the Sorbonne, where he concentrated on French language and literature.

The next couple of years were mostly spent in Paris. Quasha became friends with lots of writers like Daniel Mauroc, the early translator of Beckett into French, and Patrick Bowles, translator into English of Beckett's earliest French works. But Quasha had come to realize that, without a university degree, employment opportunities were scarce. So he was off to New York City, where he completed his undergraduate work in a year, majoring in English at New York University, while holding onto a notion that he'd be returning to Paris.

He was twenty by then, living in a $37-a-month apartment in what is now the East Village, and going to classes across town. His strategy was to attend every kind of poetry reading there was in the city, wherever that took him. Carrying his paperback Wallace Stevens with him wherever he went, he found himself increasingly immersed in the city's "experimental poetry" scene. Vibrant, exciting, it would interfere with his plan to return to Paris.

He became a regular at Café Le Métro on Second Avenue, attending its legendary readings, and striking up friendships with poets who, today, are widely admired as crucial figures in the post-war American avant-garde. These include Jerome Rothenberg, Paul Blackburn, Jackson Mac Low, Diane di Prima, David Antin, Ed Sanders, Carol Bergé, Diane Wakoski, Harold Dicker, Allen Ginsberg, and Peter Orlovsky. Quasha had to admit to himself, soon enough, that he was most at home within this more radical community.

He became friends with Anaïs Nin—having begun graduate school at NYU, studying, in particular, with M. L. Rosenthal in his legendary poetics seminars. They provided a path to the work and thinking of poets whose writings were compelling, especially those of Robert Duncan, Charles Olson, and Robert Creeley. Quasha had served as the last editor of the NYU undergraduate magazine, *Apprentice* (it had been inaugurated twenty years before by another of Rosenthal's gifted students, Paul Blackburn)—and then, as a teaching assistant, he launched the original *Washington Square Review*.

It was not that George had abandoned scholarship, however. He dove deeply into Anglo-Saxon, Middle English, and the Metaphysical poets. He also began an intense reading of Blake—with whom he has, ever since, been in a kind of dialogue. This engagement became fundamental to the young man's poetry still to come.

Quasha's academic guides, in this period, included the literary historian and former Irish politician Conner Cruise O'Brien, as well as

George Steiner (albeit their relationship had its challenging moments), and David Erdman who served as Quasha's mentor in his scholarly writing, and became a lifelong friend. Completing the M.A., and with a full-time position at SUNY Stony Brook on Long Island, for the next five years Quasha taught courses—notably in "experimental poetry," Pound, and Blake—and worked toward a doctorate at NYU.

During the Stony Brook years, Quasha got to know a sizable number of poets and artists who made visits to the campus. Among the poets who gave talks (often in Quasha's classes), read and performed, were Robert Duncan, Robert Creeley, Gary Snyder, Denise Levertov, Nicanor Parra, W. H. Auden, Kenneth Burke, and John Cage. And Quasha enjoyed close working relationships with faculty colleagues—Jim Harrison, Nam June Paik, Alfred Kazin, Jan Kott, and Lawrence Alloway.

In 1968, Stony Brook held a rather notorious poetry festival (directed by Jim Harrison and Louis Simpson). More than a hundred American poets were invited, not to give readings themselves, but to serve as audience in dialogue with a number of notable European poets such as Zbigniew Herbert, Eugene Guillevic, Czeslaw Milosz, Francis Ponge, and Eduardo de Olivera. (Some of the American poets, like Duncan and Ginsberg, didn't like not being asked to read and gave their own impromptu readings.)

With the presence of so many extraordinary poets, Quasha, assisted by Roger Guedalla and Eliot Weinberger, took the opportunity to launch *Stony Brook Journal of Poetry and Poetics*, also garnering the support of a raft of contributing editors: Robert Duncan, Jerome Rothenberg, David Antin, M. L. Rosenthal, Nicanor Parra, Hugh Kenner, Charles Simic, Kofi Awooner, Wai-Lim Yip, Michael Hamburger, Lawrence Alloway, and Jorge Carrera-Andrade. The underlying concept of *Stony Brook Journal* was to involve the diversity of poetic strands emerging in the contemporary scene and to spark a dialogue.

Summers were for returning abroad, mostly to Paris and London. Quasha paid for these trips by working as a poetry instructor on student ocean liners. The mode of travel made it easier for him to lug along a reel-to-reel tape recorder, tapes, and books. Thus, in Europe, he started recording poets and writers (inspired by Blackburn's lifelong heroic tape-recording project). Among the interviewed, in those days, were Marcelin Pleynet and Denis Roche (two members of the Tel Quel group), David Jones, and Maria Jolas (the translator of Bachelard's *Poetics of Space* and widow of Eugene Jolas). On one of these summer sojourns, Quasha spent most of an afternoon in intense conversation with the writer he most wanted to meet. Samuel Beckett welcomed him to his Paris apartment on the Boulevard Saint-Jacques. Quasha describes the experience as life-changing. "I arrived carrying two green book bags," he later recalled,

> each packed full of Beckett books for signing (one bag belonging to my English friend Roger Guedalla, also a Beckett nut). But I was so overwhelmed by his unexpected personal openness, directness, and generosity toward me that I didn't dare ask him to sign books. As I was leaving, trying to hide the embarrassingly large objects, Beckett asked, "What's in those bags?" "Oh just some books," I replied disingenuously. "I'll bet you have some books for me to sign," and he snatched them from me and dedicated each book uniquely, careful to distinguish Roger's from mine. Contrary to Martin Esslin's warning not to ask Beckett about his personal life or his critics—Esslin had facilitated the original connection for me in London—Beckett was not only talkative about his personal life but brought up issues about his critics (he mistrusted George Steiner, for example). He was surprisingly curious about what to me at the time were odd subjects; for instance, he wanted to know how things were in Harlem! I had no idea.

Quasha had heard that Beckett didn't like being recorded, so he didn't ask. No doubt those early years of recording were the seeds of what became, many years later, a monumental video artwork and ongoing archive, *art is/poetry is/music is (Speaking Portraits)*. Beginning in 2002, filmed in eleven countries to date, it includes over a thousand poets, artists and musicians. Each of them is asked to say, as impromptu as possible, what poetry, art, or music is; the artistic purpose is not reportage but intense dialogue that reveals actual creative thinking in process. The intended overall effect would be to open up, even to destabilize rather than to affirm, art definition—to see art thinking as woven in the actual life process. A 2006 Guggenheim Foundation Fellowship, in video art, helped give the project sustaining momentum.

In the early seventies, Quasha worked on an anthology he co-edited with Ronald Gross (assisted by Emmet Williams, John Robert Colombo, and Walter Lowenfels), *Open Poetry: Four Anthologies of Expanded Poems* (Simon & Schuster, 1973). In hindsight, it represents a major step toward what became Quasha's more fully conceived idea of metapoetry—poetry that, according to "Metapoetry: The Poetry of Changes," the book's introduction, "embodies specific principles of language transformation in its structural operations."

Metapoetics is resonant in his later principles: *zero point poiesis, axiality/liminality/configuration, principle-based poetics, processual singularity,* and *ecoproprioception.* These notions put forward an open, creative process unable to be fully conceptualized in advance; instead, the idea is to tap into intuitive and emergent self-organization. *Processual singularity* was no doubt helped along by Quasha's early encounters with Charles Olson (they'd first met in London, along with William Burroughs), Robert Duncan, and John Cage. Indeed, any number of others encountered at the time also might well have contributed to its further ideation, such as Louis and Celia Zukofsky, Edward Dahlberg, James Laughlin, George Oppen, and Clayton Eshleman. Even Ezra Pound figured in the developing picture.

Quasha spent an evening with Pound and Olga Rudge, thanks to James Laughlin's invitation to a private dinner. (This was when Pound had briefly returned to America from Italy, for the one and only time, to receive an honorary doctorate at Hamilton College). They got together in a Spanish restaurant in Greenwich Village. Having recently taught courses in Pound and Blake, George was anxious to ask Pound to explain why he hadn't found an ally in his predecessor, since both explicitly viewed *usura* as a main cause of social evils. Pound remained silent. Quasha pressed him: "How much did you actually read Blake?" After a substantial delay, in a resounding voice, Pound replied: "Not enough!"

Quasha's life then would take an unexpected turn. American culture was transforming itself from within. Post-war conformity was being undone by a younger generation discovering a new frontier of the mind. Quasha had resisted any connection with drugs while at Stony Brook, although students and others never ceased offering them. The stresses of being, simultaneously, a member of the university's full-time faculty at Stony Brook and a grad student at NYU—all the while editing *Stony Brook Journal*—challenged his sense of boundaries. His life choices were coming into question. Finally, he surrendered to what had seemed an alien call but in fact it was in tune with a great cultural change.

He was hardly alone at the time in his admiration for Huxley's *The Doors of Perception.* Also engaged in fervent, protracted discussions about consciousness, perception, and the nature of self with people like Alan Watts, Snyder, Duncan, and others, Quasha was feeling increasingly out of step with academic life. The opportunity came along to try mescaline. The experience of it, while on summer break visiting his family in Miami, occurred in a completely dark room. It was dramatic, to say the least; it included a powerful vision of being fully inside one of Blake's paintings, *Beatrice Addressing Dante from the Car.* The effect of Quasha's psychedelic vision was immediate and definitive. "I saw that Blake was not making 'metaphors for poetry'," he'd later say,

> but rather seeing through the veil to other dimensions of the *configurative real.* Or "metaphor," more literally, serves as a bridge to the unconfigured. Art is a threshold, a variable launching site for our "further nature" (to borrow Olson's term). From that moment, it has never seemed otherwise to me than a transformative crossing point.

Two days after the mescaline "trip," he flew to Merida, the capitol city of the Yucatan, in southern Mexico. He'd been guided there in part by his reading of Olson's *Mayan Letters*, to begin this next extended journey. He traveled overland by bus, took a boat when necessary (including an Ecuadorean military gunboat to the Galapagos), hitching rides between countries—for over a thousand miles to Chile. He arrived in Santiago on the day Allende was elected president, amidst the Chileans' celebrations as well as deep apprehensions. There he paid a visit to his friend Nicanor Parra, whose work he had recently translated during Parra's visits to Stony Brook. In George's newly evolving state of mind, everything was changing, and he was moving closer to exiting the academic orbit.

On Halloween, 1970, a few months later, he met his life partner-to-be, Susan Quasha (née Cohen). She'd been studying with Olson in Storrs, at the University of Connecticut (until he passed away). Olson told his students to get *Stony Brook Journal*. Susan's copy had failed to arrive, however, so she called about it. George agreed to bring it with him to Dr. Generosity's Bar, on Manhattan's Upper East Side, where he'd be for an afternoon poetry reading by Jackson Mac Low. Their connection was immediate, and definitive. Susan became the necessary support for what George already thought of as "a self-reorienting life. I don't see myself as an experimental poet," he said, "but as an experimental person who writes from radical life."

Six months later, the Stony Brook years were behind him. The future was wide open. George and Susan spent four months, during the summer of 1971, on an epic trip around America in a brand-new Dodge van they'd refitted with bed, books, sound, and basic kitchen supplies. First stop was a ten-day National Poetry Festival at Michigan's Grand Valley State College. Directed by Robert Vas Dias, its list of participants reads like a Who's Who of the American avant-garde then: Paul Blackburn, Robert Creeley, Robert Kelly, Armand Schwerner, Jerome Rothenberg, Gregory Corso, David Henderson, Anselm Hollo, Toby Olson, Al Young, Allen Planz, Robert Bly, Sonja Sanchez, Tom Weatherly, Diane Wakoski, Joel Oppenheimer, Ted Berrigan, Dudley Randall, and Philip Whalen. Blackburn expressed some perplexity at George's reading from a new work in progress, *Magic Spell for the Far Journey*. "You're not getting it, Paul," Creeley said, laughing. "He wants you to trip with him—it's a *far journey!*"

In a great continental circle, George and Susan headed north into Canada, looking to make contact with other poets of a radical bent. They traveled through the northwest, then southward. One remarkable stop was with Gary Snyder, at his remote Kitkiddizze residence along the Yuba River in Northern California. The week they spent there was filled with intense conversation and instruction in meditation, outside Snyder's uniquely designed house; it had been built to combine nineteenth-century logger manual design with traditional Japanese architecture, where the latter, Quasha recalls, "seemed at the crack of dawn to let its refined intimate space open wide to the rugged outdoors."

The visit marked what the Quashas viewed as a new stage in their evolving contemplative life. They flirted with the idea of buying some adjacent land, as Allen Ginsberg and others had done. Snyder's wise advice, though, was to "follow the telluric and magnetic path, and to settle where the land draws you—the right people will follow." In their minds, that path had yet to disclose itself.

They continued along the West Coast, stopping to meet with poets living in the Bay Area, Bolinas and other parts of California—Robert Creeley, David and Tina Meltzer, Ted Berrigan, Alice Notley, Ron Silliman, Phillip Lamantia. George and Susan then managed to have an intense visit with the Hopi (at a time when the Elders had begun discouraging outsiders from witnessing rituals). They met Frank Waters (the author of *Book of the Hopi*) in Santa Fe, and paid calls on Phillip Whalen and Drummond Hadley.

They returned to New York in time for the Paul Blackburn memorial at St. Mark's Church in the Bowery. The pilgrimage had proved to be a mind-reorienting period in each of their lives. They settled in Greenwich Village, taking up residence in a former lighthouse on Christopher Street, a tiny, fourth-floor walk-up apartment they'd enter from a balcony with a view of the Hudson River. They often hosted dinner parties, packing in an unlikely number of poets. Meals were prepared on their travel camping stove in the otherwise unequipped half-kitchen.

There seemed to be a steady stream of visitors as if to an unacknowledged hot spot. Charles Stein and Franz Kamin came regularly for all-night conversation. Nathaniel Tarn made it his unofficial *pied-à-terre.* The raconteur Spencer Holst lived at nearby Westbeth, like so many poets and artists. He and others felt free to stop by at will. Some came from far and wide: Raquel Jodorowsky, the Chilean poet and sister of Alejandro (whose film *El Topo* was the current midnight movie hit); Gilberto Gil, the Brazilian singer then in exile, whom George and Susan had met on the street—he'd play guitar and sing all night in the apartment; then there was the Brazilian Noigandres concrete poet, Haroldo de Campos.

Many other unexpected visitors found welcome there in that lighthouse. The tiny apartment took on a life of its own. Susan managed to wedge her pottery wheel into that small kitchen space. These early years of their lives turned out to be of immense importance in how each of them would come into their own as artists and intellectuals.

At the National Poetry Festival in Michigan, George and Jerome Rothenberg had concocted a plan—a major undertaking that would entail a year of deep reading in the archives of American poetry. They managed to uncover many obscured continental origins. The research, completed in 1973, formed the basis of what is now widely considered the foundational volume exploring those origins and their tentacles, which reach even into contemporary poetics. They titled the book, grandly, after Blake. *America a Prophecy: A New Reading of American Poetry from Pre-Columbian Times to the Present* appeared late that same year (from Random House; reissued by Station Hill Press, 2012).

Not long thereafter, Susan and George edited a book they titled (after the Poundian precedent) *Active Anthology* (Sumac, 1974). It contained work by sixty-seven poets with whom they had been in dialogue over the previous couple of years. It was in this period that George's path in poetry came fully into focus. And he has never stopped seeing the path as profoundly rooted in the most generative of his collaborations—the one with Susan.

Their early joining had been enhanced by sacredly conceived encounters with psychotropic "medicines." The first works to come out of this new life, of what was to be seen as a new species of writing, were *Amanita's Hymnal* (1971) and *A Magic Spell for the Far Journey* (1972). Each of these contained forty-three single-spaced pages, based on the notebooks George carried with him everywhere.

This notebook practice continues today, woven in a processual poetics non-separate from the current of life; however, properly speaking, it's neither personal nor biographical as such. The writing rhythmically tracks *language* events variously reflecting the interactive texture of their daily lives. Whatever reading, meditating, and dreaming is happening may also come into play, implicitly if not explicitly. Meanwhile, the writing embodies an attempt to stay aligned with entirely new kinds of awareness, always emergent. "The process of integrating the flow of insights," Quasha has said, "is often at odds with ordinary life, so it fuels the work with oscillatory tensions."

George's unique, compelling view of poetry had still fully to evolve. The main materialization of its emergence at the time was *Somapoetics: Book One* (Sumac, 1973). This book would be the first of his extended serial poems. The poems in the mode he called "Somapoeia" continued for much of a decade. A second book appeared in 1974, *Word-Yum: Somapoetics 64-69*: Seventh Series (Metapoetics Press, 1974). As of the present, roughly half of the one-hundred poem series has only been published in magazines and anthologies. These writings are the first real embodiment of what came to be called the *axial principle*, which is key to the Quasha oeuvre. A complete edition is underway.

George had begun to forge friendships that would be instrumental to his later work. These relationships of the early 1970s—most particularly with Robert Kelly, Charles Stein, and Franz Kamin—evolved into specific collaborations that are still active to this day as integral to his central, creative directions. These friendships constitute their own inflection point in the evolution of Quasha's poetics. Other poet friends from the 1970s, or even the decade before—especially David Antin, Jackson Mac Low, Jerome Rothenberg, and Dennis Tedlock—still figure in his rethinking of poetics.

Also in the early 1970s, George began his lifelong practice of t'ai chi. He was studying at Professor Cheng Man-Ch'ing's famous Shr Jung T'ai Chi School in Manhattan's Chinatown. T'ai chi created, he felt, a physical and energetic basis for the comprehension of "axiality"—a principle of self-alignment in body and mind.

In 1974, Charles Stein, Rick Fields and George became the first poets to teach at Naropa Institute (later Naropa University). There the Quashas and Stein had the opportunity to study with Chögyam Trungpa, Gregory Bateson, and the scholar and philosopher Herbert Guenther (all three consequential in the poets' thinking and practice). Besides teaching poetry at Naropa, Quasha developed a course in "Oneiropoeia," which involved, instead of retrospectively turning the dream into a poem, perpetuating the particular dream in writing, while in a post-dream liminal state. It contributed to his discovering a major benefit of a principle-based poetics: namely, that it draws upon a range of extra-literary resources (including t'ai chi, bodywork, mind training, music, visual art) as a way to get beyond cultural limitations and as an opening to the "psychonautic."

Starting in the mid 1980s, the Quashas and Stein often spent time on retreats, especially with the Tibetan teacher of Dzogchen, the late Chögyal Namhkai Norbu, among other Tibetans. It was on one such retreat, in Massachusetts in 1992, that they met the young Japanese artist Chie Hasegawa (now Hammons), who came to live for many years on their property in Barrytown, NY. In the mid-1990s, George and Chie began working on an "oneiropoetic" project of her dreams, which, over a four-year period, they collaboratively "translated" into poems. The resulting eighty poems became a volume titled *Ainu Dreams* (Station Hill Press, 1999). Through this work, George discovered further dimensions of "coperformativity in poiesis."

The intersecting vectors of his life led, additionally, to the practice of "axial bodywork," which has developed over the last forty years and initially involved professional-level training (including Craniosacral Therapy and Trager Psychophysical Integration). In the martial dimension of t'ai chi, Quasha has pointed out, "one practices 'neutralization' of contrary force (a difficult principle to grasp)," to him suggesting that he "could, with a healing intention, rather than a martial one, neutralize tension in another person's bodymind." Working physically on hundreds of others as a personal practice (at a professional level but without charging a fee) became for him a kind of contemplative laboratory for what he would later theorize as "ecoproprioception"—a view of "the boundaries of self-awareness as extending to a living field."

This has all been, moreover, a part of what has given rise to Quasha's singularly artistic/spiritual "axial stones and drawing." To be sure, one of his principal books, *Axial Stones: An Art of Precarious Balance* (North Atlantic Books, 2006), is an elaborate display of these art works. It's presented together with possibly the richest commentary on the underlying principle of his poetics.

~

In 1975, thanks to Robert Kelly, the Quashas resituated to the Hudson Valley for a one-semester teaching job George had at Bard College. After that term, he secured an NEA Fellowship in poetry; this allowed the Quashas to spend the next year on Rokeby Farm in the upstate New York region. What was meant to be a break from city life became a full-scale new way of living. They settled into their present home on Station Hill Road in the hamlet of Barrytown, with virtually the same viewing distance from the Hudson River they'd enjoyed on Christopher Street, but now ninety miles northward.

Faced with the need for a sustainable way of life outside the academy, once again, they entered the non-profit world of arts organizations. George and Susan, a marvelous artist in her own right, were able to extend the mission of Open Studio, Ltd. (originally founded by Susan and Michelle Rhodes for their ceramic work). And they established the Arnolfini Art Center in Rhinebeck, which brought new kinds of performance to the region (by Helen Adam, Meredith Monk, the Bread and

Puppet Theater, David Rattray's Artaud, Gary Hill, Jackson Mac Low, Franz Kamin, and Joe McPhee).

The art center included a print shop and design facility for writers, artists and small presses. George managed to persuade the Dutchess County government administrators to designate Open Studio as a prime employer, so that over a couple of years they received forty-seven grants from the Comprehensive Employment and Training Act (CETA); this New Deal-like program allowed the art center to employ forty-seven artists, musicians, poets, and young arts administrators, who often were sent into school programs. Eventually, the program came to serve as a first base of operations for George and Susan's own Station Hill Press.

While the art center and print facility only continued for several years, the press is still publishing books, forty-five years later. As a project of the Institute for Publishing Arts, Inc., Station Hill has produced (for over a decade, now, in partnership with poet Sam Truitt) multiple volumes widely regarded as literary milestones; they introduced, for instance, the fiction and essays of Maurice Blanchot to American readers, and revived major works of Gertrude Stein.

George's collaborations now, in the Hudson Valley, most importantly with Charles Stein and Gary Hill (the video and installation artist), are of particular importance. These have resulted in many actual collaborative works of both text and performance. From the 1970s on, Quasha and Stein developed what is now a wealth of performance works in the sound/text genre.

Rooted in earlier collaborations with Mac Low and Kamin, their newer partnerships have led to what, years later, Quasha came to call "axial music." In recent years, it has spawned The Axial Band (consisting of Stein, Quasha, and composers David Arner and John Beaulieu—at times others join in as well).

By the late 1970s, the development of an axial principle became more vivid in multi-media performance practice through Quasha's and Stein's connection with Gary Hill who had come to live on the Quasha property in Barrytown. Their many-layered performances over the years have taken place in Poland, the Czech Republic, Switzerland, the

Netherlands, and on both American coasts. The decades of collaboration yielded a pivotal collection of essays by Quasha and Stein, which explore the principle of *axiality/liminality/configuration*: *An Art of Limina: Gary Hill's Works and Writings* (Polígrafa, 2009, now available online).

George and Susan's first meeting at that poetry reading in New York City—each having come to hear Jackson Mac Low's poetry, known in part for its performance values as well as "chance operations"—stands as a fitting emblem of their intertwining lives in which art appears to modulate large forces both natural and spiritual. Friendship, and close collaboration, count as a central values in the kind of creative community that has ensued. George and Susan have been mainstays in their unique Hudson Valley community. Part of its individuality involves its geography—located close enough to New York City to be an instrumental force in the city's artistic and intellectual goings on, and far enough north of the city to have developed a collective character and outlook that owe something to the non-urban experience possible there.

Today, the Quashas engage in a wide range of fields not easy to characterize. I have wanted to acknowledge how instrumental Susan has been in all of this—while emphasizing, in this overview, George's breadth and, simply, the magnitude of his life as a whole. His poems, drawings, video productions, sculptures, music, and essays—in their originality and reach—have made a great contribution to our world of arts and ideas. He delights in extending "self-true work" to making a difference in the lives of others, as expressed preverbially in:

Things done for themselves are the only things done for all.

Maplewood, New Jersey, 2021

Zero Point Poiesis

Cover of The Daimon of the Moment (preverbs), *2015*

CARTER RATCLIFF

I: Intention, Truth, and Meaning: George Quasha's *Preverbs*

Middle things come first.

Scorned Beauty Comes Up from Behind (preverbs)

This vision has no outside, no matter how many times it's said.

Speaking Animate (preverbs)

Let each thing be until its own extinction in fullness (*she goes on*).

Verbal Paradise (preverbs)[1]

What is going on here in these selections from George Quasha's books of preverbs? Or it might be better to ask what is going by or over or under or around or through or back or toward—or choose your own preposition or adverb or adjective, at random, if you like, because these utterances destabilize the linguistic framework that often makes our word choices for us. If we're trying to say something, there is usually just one or at most a few ways to say it—if, that is, we want to be understood in familiar ways. Quasha, however, wants to be understood in unfamiliar ways. Turning always toward the moment as it turns into the future, the preverbs attain an inexhaustible freshness. Making it new, they make newness new.

Of course, newness has an ancestry, and when Quasha is asked about the preverbs' origins he usually mentions William Blake's "Proverbs of Hell" (in *The Marriage of Heaven and Hell,* 1790). This makes sense, for

[1] *Scorned Beauty Comes Up from Behind (preverbs)*, 2012, 14; *Speaking Animate (preverbs)*, 2014, 11; *Verbal Paradise (preverbs)*, 2011, 27; hereinafter cited in text parenthetically.

certain preverbs employ the tactic of reversal that shapes many of the earlier poet's proverbial declarations. In the Ten Commandments and elsewhere in Scripture, we find animadversions against lust, to which Blake replies: "The lust of the goat is the bounty of God." Moreover, "The pride of the peacock" is not a sin but "the glory of God" and "The road of excess leads" not to ruin but "to the palace of wisdom."

"Proverbs of Hell" and much else in Blake's poetry provided Quasha's preverbs with starting points—or, rather, zones rife with possibilities to be realized. Yet this talk of precedents runs the risk of obscuring more than it reveals. For there are ways in which the preverbs are nothing like "Proverbs of Hell." Though both employ the familiar grammar of sentences in English, Blake's dicta generate their persistent power to surprise not from shifts in the meanings of words but from the audacity with which they reimagine the value of that which words signify. Responding to Blake, we say, yes, lust is not a sin but a vital force. Flaunting their revaluations, Blake's Proverbs demand assent or denial. Quasha's preverbs rarely do.

Like any grammatical utterance, a preverb starts out in a direction that points to a conclusion not predictable so much as confined within a plausible range of options. And yet no preverb ends up within the bounds of plausibility. Quasha subverts the expectations built into standard syntax and semantics, or so one could say, though this interpretation ascribes to the preverbs an antagonism that they never, in my view, display. I don't see Quasha marching up to our familiar verbal habits and laying into them with the hammer of the avant-garde convention-buster. Striding forward with hardly a thought for the authority of convention, he takes each preverb to a place—an elusive place, certainly not a conclusion—where the elements of the utterance acquire the power to surprise and to tease from our bafflement a fresh sense of what things might mean.

> It's my poem when it teaches me to read from scratch.
>
> (*SB*, 21)

Offer the first four words of this preverb as a sentence to be completed and you might get: "It's my poem when it conveys my authentic voice."

Or a variation having to do with "my authentic feelings" or "my authentic being." In any case, "it's my poem when" would usually launch the project of self-definition-through-poetry that culminates in a sense of self-possession: the command of one's individual being that has been the primary goal of Western literature and art at least since the end of the eighteenth century. But this preverb does not guide us along the familiar path to that goal or to any other. It is not clear that it guides us along a path. Rather, its first four words take us from a beginning to an end that is another and more capacious beginning: the wide-open spaces of a realm whose signpost reads "from scratch."

Blake's "Proverbs of Hell" ushers us into a heaven of earthly immediacy, a liberated zone through which Quasha also ranges, with less regard for the semantic expectations set up by the syntactical patterns that initiate his preverbs. Getting to the end of a preverb, we often find that meaning has been taken not merely in an unexpected direction but in many directions at once. Nonetheless, the turns and returns—the surprises—of Blakean Proverbs prepare us to respond to the joyous complexities of this preverb.

> Time present and time past present presently.
>
> (*VP*, 33)

The affinities that link Blake and Quasha illuminate them both. However, I would like to shed a different light by comparing the preverbs to proverbs of the ordinary kind.

> It is not the function of language to say what is true.

So says a preverb from *The Daimon of the Moment.*[2] By contrast, a proverb presents itself as a truth it would be tiresome to doubt. Few would bother to find exceptions to the rule that "Birds of a feather flock together." Or that "The early bird gets the worm." And for those who find earliness uncongenial, there is "Better late than never." In those moments when "Look before you leap" is not quite right, there is "Strike while the iron is hot." Cautionary or bossy, proverbial truth is versatile

---

[2] *The Daimon of the Moment*, 2015, 11; hereinafter cited in text parenthetically.

and thus, one might think, dismissible. How can we take seriously a body of wisdom so adept at contradicting itself? Perhaps we can't and yet something worth noting lurks behind the inconsistency—and the tediousness—of proverbs.

A proverb owes its currency over the years and centuries to a strong assumption: despite the shifting incidentals of our experience, there are underlying realities that do not change. To spout a proverb is to point to some feature of a static substratum and, with the same verbal gesture, to dismiss as insignificant any fleeting contingencies that might obscure this substratum's deep and reliable stability. Appearances are one thing, realities another—an assumption with a long life. In the fifth century, the Neoplatonist Simplicius noted the sharp distinction that Parmenides drew, nearly a millennium earlier, between "the intelligible world of truth" and "the perceptible realm of appearances and seeming."[3] A mature and sober mind seeks the truth, in the hope of living in its "intelligible world." Flighty and undeveloped minds are satisfied with—or enchanted by—"appearances and seeming."

Versions of the appearance/reality opposition appear in the writings of Plato and Descartes, Aristotle and Locke and Berkeley and Kant and every other writer we call a metaphysician. In our era, an academic philosopher writes, "Metaphysics aspires to understand reality as it is in itself, independently of the conceptual apparatus observers bring to bear on it."[4] On this view, observation, no matter how conceptually sophisticated, can deliver no more than appearances; therefore, one must set observation aside and think one's way to "reality as it is in itself." How one is to do that and remain independent of one's conceptual apparatus is not clear, but never mind. The point for now is that the long tradition of Western metaphysics rests on the belief that there *is* a stable reality beneath the flicker of appearances and the further belief that this reality is knowable, if only in principle. Crucial to the metaphysical enterprise, these beliefs

[3] Parmenides, "The Way of Opinion," quoted by Simplicius, *Early Greek Philosophy*, ed. Jonathan Barnes (New York: Penguin Books, 1987), 137.

[4] Stephen Yablo, "Identity, Essence, and Indiscernibility" (1987), *Metaphysics*, ed. Jaegwon Kim and Earnest Sosa (Oxford: Blackwell, 1997), 122.

supply proverbs with whatever authority they possess. Thus, to utter a proverb is to make a drastically condensed metaphysical argument.

Arguments of this kind employ threadbare metaphors, not coherent trains of thought, and, as we have seen, they come in roughly contradictory pairs. "Fools rush in where angels fear to tread." All right, but what about "Fortune favors the brave"? Fitting readymade formulas to transient moments, the mind given to proverbs makes metaphysical points in a casual, opportunistic manner. The results are of course not philosophy but rhetoric, which Aristotle defines as "the faculty of observing in any given case the available means of persuasion."

Whatever form they may take from one occasion to the next, the devices of rhetoric fall under the broad headings of *ethos* (the perceived character, hence the credibility, of the speaker or writer); *pathos* (the audience's capacity for emotional response); and *logos* (the argument that the rhetorician presents).[5] Deploying this triad, rhetoricians try to persuade us that they have grounded their arguments on the bedrock truth that appearances are thought to hide. When Quasha states in a preverb previously quoted that "It is not the function of language to say what is true," he could be understood as taking up a stance of head-on opposition not only to the everyday metaphysics—the rhetoric—of the proverb but also to the ancient metaphysics that undergirds much contemporary philosophy. But this reading of the preverbs construes them too schematically.

There are two alternatives to truth: lies and fictions. Nothing in Quasha's preverbs counts as a lie. Nor do they display the signs of fiction. Must we then conclude that, one of his preverbs to the contrary, they aspire to tell truths? Yes, but just as Quasha loosens and sometime unties the bonds of standard syntax and semantics, so he throws our routine notions of truth off balance. Though they originate in the immediacies of experience, the preverbs do not make observations that are in any ordinary way verifiable. A preverb does not offer truth with the aura of fact. Rather, it follows the impulse to speak truly into regions where truth is not revealed, readymade, but emerges from the effort to find meaning in the preverb's play of language.

[5] Aristotle, *Rhetoric*, 1355b, 1356a.

Living in the fluid present it creates for itself, a preverb neither asserts nor denies the static, underlying truths of metaphysics. Nor do these writings celebrate or deplore the realm of appearances. The preverbs are beyond the reach, the authority, of the appearance/reality opposition and any other binary scheme we might bring to bear. As we read a page of preverbs, even the writer/written work dichotomy begins to wobble and dissolve, only to reform and become, once more, elusive. This is clearest when we look for Quasha's intention, that seemingly crucial element in the character—the *ethos*—of a writer or a speaker.

With its obsessive focus on individuality, modernity vexed the matter of the author's intention so thoroughly that certain literary critics chose to dismiss it. In judging the meaning and value of a poem, they said, only the text on the page is to be considered. This formalist program is nowhere more clearly set forth than in "The Intentional Fallacy" (1946) by W. K. Wimsatt and Monroe C. Beardsley. Their essay still has a bracing force all these decades later—and provides a precedent for the attacks on the traditional idea of authorship made more recently by Roland Barthes and others. The problem with banishing individual intention is the blank spot that appears in its place. A literary work doesn't simply coalesce, like frost on a windowpane. However powerfully writers may be directed by the authority of language, culture, and society, nothing gets written unless someone intends to write it. Even the arch-formalists Wimsatt and Beardsley acknowledged that, in making sense of a poem, we have no choice but to "impute" its "thoughts and attitudes" to someone with the intention of conveying precisely those "thoughts and attitudes." Their nomination for this role was a fictional character: "the dramatic speaker" implied by the poem and to be carefully distinguished from the person who happened to have written it.[6]

But how fictional is George Quasha, the writer whose voice is recognizable in each of the many preverbs? A further question: what would we gain by choosing either Quasha the flesh-and-blood person or a

[6] W. K. Wimsatt and Monroe C. Beardsley, "The Intentional Fallacy" (1946), *The Verbal Icon: Studies in the Meaning of Poetry* (Lexington, KY: The University Press of Kentucky, 1954), 5.

make-believe Quasha on the model of Wimsatt and Beardsley's "dramatic speaker"? If we opt for the actual person, we must define the preverbs as self-expression and say, in effect, that Quasha with these utterances intends to communicate some thought or feeling. To opt for the "dramatic speaker" is to transpose self-expression to the world of a fictional character. I suppose it's impossible to disprove these theories of the preverbs, and yet it would be difficult to herd the following into the exegetical corral where the process of extracting a message takes place.

> Touch tells you one surface is not one mind.[7]

Confronted with this preverb, common sense might bluntly ask: who needs to be told that "one surface is not one mind"? Of course it is not, no one ever said it was, so what's the point? To get beyond a dead-end question like this, we must set aside the idea that touch—or the entire preverb—wants to *tell* us anything. Or that there is anything else of a sharply focused nature that the preverb wants to do. Using the standard form of a declarative sentence to put "touch," "surface," "mind" into ambiguous, intersecting orbits, invites us to understand these words as providing one another with heretofore unimagined contexts. From new contexts emerge new meanings—or so we are persuaded to imagine. What if this preverb is persuading the mind/body problem to glide into a fresh configuration? Is that possible? In other words, is it imaginable that an utterance might direct its rhetorical energies not at a reader, not at a listener, but at a set of concepts? On what occasion would that be persuasive?

That every rhetorical situation is inescapably particular brings into play the notion of *kairos*: the opportune moment. A rhetorician successful by the usual standards knows what to say and when to say it. It may be the case that "great minds think alike" or "fine words butter no parsnips," yet neither bit of wisdom would be welcome when milk is spilled. In the world presupposed by the metaphysics of proverbs, *kairos* is a simple matter: it is time to intone a proverb when some easily recognized aspect of the Real becomes salient. As an irreparable accident prompts talk of spilt milk, so we are told to "fight fire with fire" when the need for a vigorous

[7] *Glossodelia Attract (preverbs)*, 2015, 83.

counterattack is obvious. By contrast, no obvious occasion inspires any of Quasha's preverbs. Follow the switchbacks and grand leaps of

> Recalling the lost wording reclaims the call of origin.
>
> (*DM*, 71)

and you are brought to a place where it becomes intuitable that *kairos* for Quasha has nothing to do with seizing an opportunity and everything to do with striding verbally beyond any concern for the opportune. Ushering us out of those realms of experience shaped by precedent and expectation, a preverb is not a response to an occasion. It gives birth to its occasion. Or it is the occasion and, if so, all certainty about Quasha's intention vanishes and we wonder what his connection to this occasion—the preverb—might be.

Literally speaking, the preverbs appear when he writes them down. But who or what is *he*? Displaying no interest in setting himself up as a sender of messages, a fount of wisdom, or a purveyor of insights, the "George Quasha" we acknowledge as the author of the preverbs puts neither Authenticity with a capital "A" nor Truth with a capital "T" at stake. So there is no need to locate and certify a True and Authentic Quasha as the source of the preverbs, which emerge from a region to which we may well have as much access as he does. These sentences take their sometimes ungraspable form in the space between him and language. Or between him and us, a space alive with any number of others. With *Hilaritas Sublime* that milling crowd increases by one.[8]

A sequence of George Quasha's preverbs appears to the right of a photograph by Susan Quasha in each of this book's two-page spreads. Her thirty-four images awaken us to the variety of the visible world and, just as important, to the various stances we take toward the myriad things we see. With every juxtaposition of visual and verbal, photographer and writer take the opportunity to sail past the temptation to illustrate or to provide a caption. In response to Susan's image of a wide, frozen river, with silhouetted mountains beyond, George writes

---

[8] George Quasha and Susan Quasha, *Hilaritas Sublime*, 2020.

The picture I'm getting didn't feel like me yesterday.
I am here for my picture.

("Captive Provision," *Hilaritas Sublime,* 30)

How, you might ask, is Susan's photograph George's picture? It doesn't depict him, nor does he own it. Indeed, the interplay of these two lines carries him past questions of representation and ownership to the idea of getting the picture—understanding something—which morphs into the further idea of self-awareness, of noting how it feels to feel like oneself.

Like other feelings, this one is mutable, hence the constitutive bond that joins the self-aware self to a provisionally understood world is never static, not for an instant. And so there is an irony to be read into Susan's picture of the river. Yes, this body of water is frozen but her deployment of tone and point of view gives the image an inexhaustible complexity. You can't memorize its pattern of gleam and flicker; it changes with each attentive look, as George changes from day to day—but not utterly. Self-awareness sustains, among other things, the continuity that permits him to compare how he is "here"—today—with how he was "yesterday."

Susan presents long shots, close-ups, and photos focused on the middle distances. Though her focus is usually sharp, she sometimes she lets flowing water or some other moving subject throw the image out of focus; on other occasions, blurring is the work of her own, perhaps intentionally jittery hand. After centering a photograph on a discrete object, she might, in another moment, record not the lineaments of an object but a field of texture. Usually, it is possible to put a name to her subject—a patch of pavement, for example, or a sunset. When it is not, we may well turn to a metaphorical reading. Though the grid in the sixteenth photograph is too watery and shimmering to identify with ease, it is not so much easy as inevitable that we will see this as an image of becoming or, at the very least, of one state turning into another. As George says in one of the lines facing this photograph, "Identity gets slippery."

Facing pages from Hilaritas Sublime *(2020), photography Susan Quasha/preverbs George Quasha*

3 *sky acts*

Feeling discrimination here
and it's coming from outside
the periphery of my knowing circle.
The Pre-Pre-Socratic Sayings of Ontononymous the Particular[1]

If it comes from everywhere it *is* everywhere as plain as we plainly see.
It's as right as you stay with.

Clouds teach breaking the mold you most wish to hold.
Mid lane is mid sentence from beginning to end.

Some principles are true to the extent you cannot rectify their differences.
A true line is about following what you know can't be followed anyway.

When I talk environment voice goes both ways at once.
Some things you don't talk about you just talk along.

Midway is the best time to look up.
Long inside dense formulation gives of sudden sense beauty never formulated.

Sky writes real according to your philosophy.
Real says so if you're hearing right.

Reality is my number one project.
Think it skyish foretaste of the present making a path.

Its poiesis excitedly fails to take control of significance.
The line disperses as it draws out drawing on out.
It changes changing everything.

---

[1] Hereafter attributed as "Ontononymous."

Unaccompanied by Susan's photographs, George's many preverb sequences remake and reremake familiar relationships between language and its referents. In old-style mimesis, this was the relationship between a mirror and whatever it reflects. With the advent of the Age of Sensibility, in the eighteenth century, poets turned the mirror on themselves, evoking their inwardness with images taken from the external world. Then, as this familiar story takes us to the early decades of the next century, poetry turned more militantly self-reflective, soaring from sensibility to the full-fledged Romanticism that led John Keats to describe William's Wordsworth's mode as "the egotistical sublime."[9] A monumental egotist himself, Keats got this precisely right; moreover, he continued Wordsworth's policy, inherited from Thomas Gray, Thomas Warton, and other poets of Sensibility, of recruiting external appearances—bits and pieces of observable Nature—to serve as vehicles of self-expression. Modernism began when Théophile Gautier proclaimed that a poem must not traffic in humanity's shared Truths or the glories of Nature or the poet's unique being. Its only legitimate interest is in its own, self-sufficient beauty.[10] The critic Victor Cousin was the first to call this new and stand-offish aesthetic "art for art's sake."[11]

---

[9] John Keats, letter to Richard Woodhouse, October 27, 1818, *Letters of John Keats to His Family and Friends*, ed. Sidney Colvin, London: MacMillan and Company, 1925, 184.

[10] This comment implies that Modernism breaks with Romanticism, a defensible proposition, yet I ought to acknowledge that certain styles and movements usually gathered under the Modernist label—Expressionism, for example, and Surrealism—are updated versions of Romanticism.

[11] "L'art pour l'art," the phrase we translate as "art for art's sake," appeared first in Victor Cousin's *Lectures on the True, the Beautiful, and the Good* (1818, published 1854). See *Art in Theory 1815-1900: An Anthology of Changing Ideas*, ed. Charles Harrison and Paul Wood, with Jason Gaiger, Oxford: Blackwell, 1998, 192. The most influential of the early formulations of "art for art's sake" or "pure art" is to be found in Théophile Gautier, "Preface to Mademoiselle de Maupin" (1835), reprinted in *Strangeness and Beauty: An Anthology of Aesthetic Criticism*, 2 vols., ed. Eric Warner and Graham Hough (Cambridge University Press, 1983), vol. 1, 157-67.

Cousin coined that phrase more than two centuries ago. There is no question of mapping, however sketchily, the myriad variations on art for art's sake that have appeared since then, though it is safe to say that no one, in any medium, has managed to break every bond between art and the world. Every painting, however abstract, is at least residually representational. A poem can flaunt its refusal to refer to anything beyond the text and yet, if it employs recognizable words, it cannot help making tenuous reference to something that is not the poem itself. Still, I can imagine my talk of art for art's sake prompting the thought that Quasha's indifference to traditional notions of Truth and Authenticity has taken detachment from the world to a new extreme: defying our hope of a coherent meaning or stable value, we must appreciate his preverbs as bits of language isolated in their self-referential purity. But the opposite is the case.

Rather than detach poetic utterance from the shared world of ordinary experience, the preverbs show us a new way for poetry to be there, deep in the world's manifold—and thus he has given poetry a new way to address us. With *Hilaritas Sublime* that address has become more complex, for it puts two mediums into play. Each medium—language and photography—engages not only the world but also the other medium, implying in the process the possibility of bringing further mediums into play and ultimately revamping the world and one's ways of being in it—or, to make the point from another angle, revamping our understanding of our experience, in isolation and in one another's company. With its verbal-visual mix, *Hilaritas Sublime* produces an extraordinary amount of speculative energy, all of it swirling us at the speed of intuition into regions favorable to our own speculations about being and becoming, self and world, time and memory, intention and meaning, and, needless to say, more.

There is no end to looking into the play of language and image in *Hilaritas Sublime.* Slipping the bonds of expectation and habit, this book neither demands that we plunge into its unchartable currents nor reproaches us if we can't manage to do so. No collaboration of visual and verbal artists could be less prescriptive than this one. Rather than pressure us to acknowledge its coherence, it invites us to grapple with its openness, as gracefully as possible. If something like a meaning emerges, that is all to the good. The greater good is in the grappling itself.

to wake one stone wears another

Axial Stones #4 with preverb, 2006

Carter Ratcliff

II: Axial Art[1]

Gathered into one another's company, George Quasha's Axial Stones establish a zone of riveting stillness. Yet each was brought to that shared state by a history—a tempo of events—entirely its own. It is the work of an instant to spot a likely stone, but it may take the artist days or years to see how two stones fit together to form a single piece. The fitting itself can be quick or slow. In any case, the process follows strict rules: one stone must be balanced on another, at a narrow point of contact, and no adhesive is permissible nor may either stone be modified in any way. The results are astonishing.

At first glance, it looks as if Quasha has found a batch of wildly eccentric natural objects. Then one realizes, with a start, what one is seeing. In each case, not one but two objects have been joined at precisely the point that turns them into a unity. These configurations appear to be sturdy. Yet each is so delicately balanced that the slightest touch would topple it. Their collective title, *Axial Stones*, draws attention to the axes around which all of them must, out of deference to gravity, be organized. Most axes—the axis of the earth, for example, or the crossed axes of a Beaux Arts building—are not only clear but stable and, we hope, permanent. The axes of the Axial Stones are different: clear and for the moment stable but charged with an air of contingency. Uninterested in the sort of axis that enforces solidity, Quasha finds ones that look alive with precarious-ness. Thus he collaborates in a redefinition of art that was launched by John Cage, his favorite predecessor, and might be understood, in brief, as a dismissal of Plato, who dismissed art as derivative.

In the *Republic* and elsewhere, Plato argued that painters and sculptors make images of perishable and earthly things that are themselves

[1] Originally published as the foreword to *Axial Stones: An Art of Precarious Balance*, 2006; hereinafter cited in text parenthetically. The foreword extends a review in *Art in America* of Quasha's 2004 exhibition at the Manfred Baumgartner Gallery in New York's Chelsea district.

inadequate images of imperishable models, ideal Forms residing in a heaven beyond the reach of human intellect. Plotinus insisted that art can show us those Ideas, those absolute Realities, and for nearly two millennia artists adapted his faith to their eras. Though transience is the subject of the Impressionist painters, the structures of their pictures are no less stable than those of the Academics who preceded them and the geometric abstractionists—Mondrian and company—who came after them. As crucial as it is to harmonious composition, that stability does not reveal a transcendent order. Yet it is an emblem of the yearning for transcendence, and it remains intelligible. Plotinus still haunts us with ghostly encouragement to believe that art is representation and the best art represents the highest things.

As the middle of the twentieth century approached, John Cage suggested that a work of art need not be a picture of anything. It can be the trace of an action or the action itself. Early in the 1950s, Harold Rosenberg invented the figure of the American Action Painter. Toward the end of the decade, Allan Kaprow proposed that painters set aside their brushes and enter three-dimensional space as instigators of Happenings. This flurry of art-as-activity was stilled for a moment by the sudden, blunt immobility of the Minimalist object. Then several of the Minimalists and many younger artists shifted their attention to the process of making things. Process itself became the focus for them that it had long been for Cage. Process art, performance art, real-time video art—all these and more freed art from its ancient hope of revealing absolutes. To acknowledge action is to flirt with contingency or, in Quasha's case, to embrace it without reserve. Or it may be that he induces it to embrace him.

To make the *Axial Stones*, he must use two hands. This is obvious and worth mentioning only in light of the process that results in the Axial Drawings. When he draws, Quasha works with both hands simultaneously. Dragging the edges of his graphite sticks over the paper in quick, curving motions, he produces elegant swirls of translucent gray. Though these images look as if they might vanish as quickly as they came into being, each is anchored by the presiding line that emerges from the pulse of Quasha's gesture. The Axial Drawings bring the clarity of an axis into delicately felt balance with idiosyncratic forms, as the *Axial Stones* do in three dimensions. Of course, the balance of the Stones is literally precarious and that of the graphite forms is not. Beyond this difference is everything that the Stones and Drawings have in common: grace, an acceptance of contingency, and the two-handedness of the processes that generate them. Consciously or not, we gather from every work of art an intuition of a bodily state. Ambidextrously improvising, Quasha endows his work with a limber, responsive sense of the body—his body, in particular, and all bodies, not so much in general as in their specific potential.

Axial Drawing, Dakini Series (7 acrylic paints, 4 brushes, two-handed), 2016

Quasha's bodily sense finds its most telling contrast in Leonardo's image of Vitruvian Man, which aligns the human form with the symmetries of circle and square. Invoking the authority of the Roman architect Vitruvius, Leonardo declared that the proportions of the body are not only compatible with geometric form but reflect the structure of the universe. To make his analogy between micro- and macrocosm as persuasive as he could, he depicted the body front-on with a strictly vertical axis for a backbone. This anatomical symmetry reappears in buildings, in city plans, and in traditionally composed pictures—and elsewhere, too, for we like to project our cosmological notion of the body onto the world around us. It comforts us to see our structure mirrored by our surroundings. Yet we enjoy this comfort at the price of a drastic generalization, for Vitruvian Man is an abstraction: no one in particular.

A yearning to transcend one's particular self animates much of Western culture. Or we try to have it both ways, as in Expressionist art, which claims that the way to the universal is through the individual. As I noted, it has only been in the past half century or so that artists have given up the transcendental bootstrapping that began with Plotinus. To put it the other way around, they have plunged without reservation into their particular circumstances. Of course, the allure of the universal persists. Only some artists—really, just a few—have followed John Cage to a full acceptance of contingency. Outstanding among them is George Quasha, whose axial art makes it clear that an immersion in the flux of experience is not a submission to happenstance. For Quasha, an axis is like an intention: a force that, as it generates possibilities, gives them a provisional but intelligible order. Every esthetic advances a hope, for truth or clarity or beauty or whatever. Quasha's esthetic is driven by the hope that possibility will always be open and fresh, never predictable. Thus will our possibilities remain human, thoroughly ours and in no need of transcendental alibis.

Gary Shapiro

George Quasha: Words of Wonder

> Follow the bouncing thought.
> It's not an it even to itself.
> Mind shows when the flow is knowing.[1]

"Wonder further!" This imperative surfaces in *Verbal Paradise*, the first text in George Quasha's "preverbs." I would like to hear it as a call, somewhat in the vein of Heidegger and his more acute readers (say, Foucault and Derrida for starters) to think the unthought. Philosophy begins in wonder, as Aristotle says, but Quasha reminds us that thought and writing should persist in wonder, pushing the borders of the wonder-ful, being open to the future (*a-venir*), the e-vent, and the stranger, the unpredictable and incalculable, that which will arrive. Arrivals take many proliferating forms and shapes, as Quasha limns in his adventures with the luminal, the axial, the verbal and preverbal.

Perhaps it's my professional deformation, but Quasha's preverbs especially put me in mind of the gnomic sayings of the "dark philosopher" Heraclitus of Ephesus (no doubt others will think of the *Tao te Ching* or other texts). Heraclitus allowed Greek to speak in a memorably enigmatic way that has entranced and puzzled for 2500 years. "Listen not to me, but to the *logos*," he instructs us, in a saying that requires us to do both, and then to think about its performative complexity. Or "Follow the bouncing thought." The word or thought (and *logos*) swings both ways, keeps things moving, a pervasive rhythm, wave, vibration rather than an inert, fixed and stable meaning. (Words should not be kept in stables or confined by digital writing programs.) Just as we might be led through a song's screened text by a bouncing ball, let's give ourselves over

[1] "Woman at the Heart of it All," *Glossodelia Attract (preverbs)*, 2015, 5; hereinafter cited in text parenthetically.

to the thoughts that continue to expand, advance in new directions, or unexpectedly double back. There are words behind and beneath words. Quasha calls them preverbs, an archaic, originary language.

This is not in the sense of the most ancient or with the most distinguished pedigree, but rather the *logos* that moves through all things, or the "bouncing thought." An archi-writing, to adopt Derrida's locution, Quasha's thought—or shall we say the thought that seizes him?—bounces along in a jolly mood as it plays with paradox. Some bounces may bring us up short. "It's not an it even to itself," he writes. We want to name, identify, articulate, and classify the bouncing thought, the moving *logos*.

We'd like to think of it as an *it*. But there's no it there; it's process all the way down. The repetition of "it," "it's," repetition, as Foucault observed of Andy Warhol's soup cans or multiple Marilyn lips, is an emptying out of meaning, a self-consuming mantra. "It" is pre-verbal, not in the sense of being silent or dumb, but in enabling, opening up a space for words to play, to flourish, to open themselves and find meanings we and they never suspected.

"Mind shows when the flow is knowing." All things flow. We do and do not step twice into the same river. Flowing can be knowing, and knowing (or *gnosis*) is always flowing. "Mind shows": not that "mind" sits back on the sidelines and pronounces judgment to confirm that knowledge has been achieved, but rather that mind flares up; it shows itself, makes an appearance, when the flowing is a knowing. Thoughts are not in me, but I am in thought, said Charles Peirce when he was deconstructing Descartes' mental substance.

Showing itself—this is an exemplary case of the middle voice, neither active nor passive, that runs through the bouncing thoughts and volatile thoughts that Quasha allows to speak out. Greek is a philosophical language; among other reasons, because of its well-developed middle voice. Some colloquial Anglophone analogues: "the situation unfolds," "shit happens." Phenomenology is a triumph of the middle voice. Heidegger lets phenomenology happen by recalling that the middle voice Greek *phainesthai* should be translated as "it shows itself." The phenomenon is neither subject nor object. For Quasha language emerges and shows itself in preverbs.

> Shine through or see through or more.
> Every two is manyer than you think and a splitting *y* in the middle.
> We fork by nature.
>
> ("Speaking Animate," *GA*, 12)

There is a truly wonderful, wonder-inducing, generative, and originary dimension. But can one speak of a dimension of the unmeasurable? Shining and seeing in this verbal paradise are always plural. If "man" is "a poor, bare, forked animal" (as Lear says), then the forking is "manyer," always a multiplying. Every two is more than two. To see only two roads diverging is short-sighted. Someone said: "There are two kinds of people, those who divide everything into two and those who do not." The forking continues, we're happy to wonder and wander further in Quasha's verbal paradise.

Cheryl Pallant

Poetry Saying

George Quasha has a poetic way of saying what is so and isn't so and is something else. Which can confuse and irritate readers preferring to rest on the laurels of understanding and knowledge. His poetry will have none of it, and his poetry will have all of it, certainty trembling in a turn of word or phrase, a line or poem later, leaving the reader coming and going in a syntactic and semantic tug of war that has no winner unless we loosen readerly expectations of grasping after knowing as stable and lasting.

To read Quasha's books of preverbs is to read in a state of suspended animation and arbitration, a self-mockery that is both annihilation and preservation. He refers to his process as *axiality* which "is not a thing: not a philosophy; not a religion; not an aesthetic; in short, not itself any of the many ways that can be used to understand it. It's more like a space..."[1]

Reading any volume of his preverbs is akin to trying to remember a dream upon waking or holding water in your hand. Slippage in understanding is inevitable. Looking too closely yields shimmers of conclusiveness which are subject to change. Best to look askew.

> Nothing is the way it's always been said.
>
> Working language means cutting through to secret holdings.[2]

Best to read by alternating the lobe reserved for reading with the lobe that generates dreams. His is a poetry of the corpus collosum, the meeting place of brain hemispheres, a hub for sensing, an axis mundi of the many parts of ourselves. His is a cyclical poetry of proprioception meeting pulse meeting listening meeting word meeting proprioception and onward and onword.

---

[1] George Quasha, Prologue to *Axial Stones: An Art of Precarious Balance*, foreword Carter Ratcliff, 2006, 20; hereinafter cited in text parenthetically.

[2] *Glossodelia Attract (preverbs)*, 2015, 10; hereinafter cited in text parenthetically.

We're here for the ride but who knew such fractals....

Every tongue tip waves particle internals eternal, so to say.

Stuttering mouth quakes its own evolution.[3]

What is known shines as true for a moment, the beacon shifting with a consequent breath, word, line, or stanza. Nothing stays or says as so for long. Poems abound in word play not for the sake of trickery, but as a way to highlight shifts in language and being always taking place moment to moment, making what may otherwise go unnoticed noticeable.

Our proprioceptions are too subtlebodied to track fully conscious,
all wise open.[4]

Consciousness is tricky business and Quasha games the system by naming and pulling the curtain aside to reveal the moves within mind, which include language with its undertow. What's left is balancing between looking at and looking away, concentrating and wandering off, consciousness conversing with the unconscious.

Preverbs balance between poles, in the friction and tension between space that is empty and space that is full, between saying something is so through words that define and showing those same words faltering under the weight of their defining constraints. Words hold a place on the line and then loosen. His poetry lives where constructs of meaning come and go, where words write him onto a line and definitions slide. The dream evaporates, water drips from the hand, and words or lines meaning one thing assume new meaning. It's not that his language refuses to say. In fact, it excels again and again in declarative lines that espouse insights, but it's a reach that delivers the goods while also questioning the delivery.

Every phrase becomes suspect. Declarations acknowledge shortcomings while asserting otherwise.

---

[3] *Verbal Paradise (preverbs)*, 2011, 24; hereinafter cited in text parenthetically.

[4] *The Daimon of the Moment (preverbs)*, 2012, 40; hereinafter cited in text parenthetically.

The strangeness of impossible naming is inescapable.[5]

Every phrase asserts its note, then backs away, coming forth anew soon after, a complete cycle, creation in the process of creating. Words rise up from the silence, from the dream of a body tuned to the subtleties of proprioception. Stanzas unfold a gnostic passage in continual sequential making and unmaking as potent as a breath and as lasting.

Preverbs create an open space like what occurs in improvisation where creating requires no anticipation, no preplanning, only showing up ready to manifest impulses. This open space is available in meditation when thought falls away, the conceptual and critical mind quiets, and the soundless hum sounds tranquility. A similar space is established by the trained body worker's hands entering the field of a client's body and landing upon the skin, listening without judgement to what the body transmits. Here is the axial space where energies both static and in motion converge and a self aware of itself looks by looking away, and a poet writes by letting the writing have its way with him, the motion of linguality allowing quiescence.

> Here I enter a site where I can negotiate with words for the release
> of mind.
>
> Explaining the text is like complaining to God.
>
> It hurts to word it.
>
> Everything said has chargeback to the body.
>
> (*DM*, 44)

Axiality might also go by the name of the "still point," a term used by osteopaths to refer to the temporary cessation of the craniosacral rhythm of the spine, a profound rest that instigates healing and perception of wholeness. Preverbs show a similar oscillating of rhythms, words vibrat-

---

5 *Things Done For Themselves (preverbs)*, 2015, 48; hereinafter cited in text parenthetically.

ing with syntactic and semantic shifts. Preverbs reveal a wholeness that arises out of deep language listening, a focus poised on an edge of emergence, an awareness and reliance on language along with recognizing its unreliability and mutability.

Quasha's preverbs live in a space of presence where everything quivers with impermanence. Any reflective process is partial. Lines admit as much, a prevalence of paradox. Engage with the path of his words but prepare, too, for disorientation which leads to a new orientation.

> First comes unreading ending rereading with reading between.[6]

Quasha is continually falling down the rabbit hole, welcoming the free fall of awareness in writing that sustains an axial consciousness.

> The eye with which it sees the page is the eye with which the
> poem sees you.
>
> It can't stop paraphrasing itself.
>
> (*DM*, 70)

The process of writing preverbs calls for a centering of body, speech, and mind, an ego aligning with personal and collective influences and surrendering to the upwelling of language. While writing, he lives on the poetic line, the writing moving through him as if channeled. Words speak up on the line and tell him (and us) what is so before the line moves everyone along. He is a willing participant in the liberating power of poetry as a form, at home with mutability and the ineffable.

> As I was writing the words said this is where life knows it takes
> place through me.
>
> Sudden turmoil, another meaning's rippling across everything I've
> ever laid pen to.

---

[6] *Strange Beauty by Stranger Attraction (preverbs),* the second series in an unpublished manuscript, *Hearing Other (preverbs)*, 2018, 13; hereinafter cited in text parenthetically.

> I'm surfacing. Resurfacing. New face facing. Surfing for face.
>
> (*GA*, 78)

The relative self with a specific body and identity bows down to universal principles. He recognizes self not as a noun but a verb. The body of his texts shows selfing, a moment to moment generating of subtleties of self through language. Interestingly, Quasha regularly refers to the poetic urge and sometimes the poems themselves as feminine. I can't help but think about the *Shekinah*, the feminine appearance of the divine, a godly upwelling, the immanence or fleshing out of the immaterial, for him breath and energy manifesting as word. This feminine poetic impulse is presented with sensual and sexual overtones.

> Using your lingual reflex she lassoes your linguality well nigh
> bronco busting.
>
> The tongue gets kicked around no matter what.
>
> (*GA*, 12)

Rather than assign the feminine the traditional sense of feeling (versus masculine thinking), I put forth the feminine as embodying being. Being has no plan other than to exist, to flow and arise, urging the tongue to wrap around the flux of words. The feminine stands in contrast with the repetitive structure of the more masculine declarative lines and their appearance of stable knowing. The tension and play between them generates axiality. A precarious knowing and balance occurs in the between space, the liminal that is constantly shifting.

The feminine/masculine interplay also corresponds to the left and right side of the brain. A similar interplay between hemispheres occurs with the two-handed technique Quasha employs for his acrylic dakini series that serves as the covers for his volumes of preverbs.

So much depends upon his lines in constant tussle for positioning, the drone of repetition and embrace of opposites generating a restlessness that creates rest. They suggest, too, a unitive consciousness where differentiating subject from object and the poet from the poems becomes difficult. Preverbs seek knowing through unknowing, being through misdirection and redirection, a koanic path that leads nowhere and everywhere.

Preverbs get by through continually unsaying the sayable. Opposites attract on his lines and "hold the void but shapely" (*SBSA* 35). Preverbs take us on a pursuit of the unachievable, pointing out the efficacy and deficiency and defiance and celebration of poetry. The way into his poems is a way out of poetry and back into something new. They are distinctively Quasha poking holes in poetry and bowing deeply.

Axial Drawing, Dakini Series (7 acrylic paints, 4 brushes, two-handed), 2013

stones stutter to a balance

Axial Stones #19 with preverb

Edward S. Casey

I
Quasha at the Edge

> A stone at the edge is still happening
>
> *Axial Stones*

> Precarious balance is the prayer of the edge.
>
> "Breaking Wave," *Verbal Paradise (preverbs)*[1]

1

George Quasha brings poetry and sculpture to their respective edges—each to its own edge, and by a unique twist both together. In this brief tribute to that singular double accomplishment, I shall explore the sense of edge ingredient in Quasha's sculptural and poetic works—a sense that is both like and unlike. I will end by a brief discussion of the "absolute edge," a term that suggests the farther limits of Quasha's thought: on the very edge of theology.

Quasha's remarkable axial stone sculptures are explorations in edge-work. When one stone is precariously balanced against, or better with, another, at least two edges touch. Not two surfaces: as would be the case when sheerly smooth stones with flat surfaces are aligned with each other, surface-to-surface. But when the surfaces are irregular, as in virtually every stone sculpture created by Quasha, they connect at discrete edge-points. (By "edge-point," I mean the discrete place where a given edge provides a point of possible contact with another such edge.) A particular edge-point figures into the balancing of stones in Quasha's deft

---

[1] *Axial Stones: An Art of Precarious Balance*, foreword Carter Ratcliff, 2006, 38; *Verbal Paradise (preverbs)*, 2011, 36; hereinafter cited in text parenthetically.

hands. These hands, guided by agile eyes, determine the edge-points in each of two (sometimes more) stones. Between these edge-points there is an equipoise sufficient to last indefinitely and to form a single axis for the contiguous stones.

In this bold action, edges cease to be merely the places where a certain material substance like that of stones runs out—to be just the *edges of* that substance, its outer limits. Quasha's intervention in the life of stones surpasses this plebian sense of edge by discovering and thematizing those edges whose exclusive raison d'être is to be the agents of affiliation between otherwise unwieldy or uninteresting stones found strewn in rivers and streams—remnant stones, cast off from prehistoric sedimentary or volcanic events. The earth's *rejecta* become the very materials of Quasha's transforming presence. This presence and these raw lithic things interreact in the fulcrum of the edge. The alignment of effective edges constitutes the *axis mundi* of axial stones.

We are now in a position to grasp the meaning of Quasha's enigmatic sentence (cited above as an epigram): "a stone at the edge is still happening...." At the edge of a stone an event happens if this edge can concatenate in the right way with the edge of another stone. Such a happening in time arises from the juxtaposition of stones in space. It forms an "actual occasion," in Whitehead's term, for a nexus in which unfolding in time and extension in space occur at once, coalescing in one moment, coming together in what we conventionally call an "event." In the case of axial stones a geological event "still happens" in that Earth in motion causes everything on it to also be in motion and subtly changing, and sooner or later balanced things will fall. Thus they are continuing to occur, though now as re-configured by Quasha's artistry, which he views as a collaboration with the stones. And it happens as *still*, not moving in itself—as the rock-bound equivalent of "the still point of the turning world."[2] Except that there is no consistent center here around which a world could turn—no center locatable outside the event of balancing; rather, the center as plumbline enacted, indeed discovered, in the moment of stones coming together, creates instead an apparently decentered, off-center balancing act, which, by virtue of a plumbline you

[2] T.S. Eliot, "Burnt Norton," *Four Quartets* (New York: Harcourt, 1943).

cannot see, puts stones back in a still position: as still as artworks that consist in the arrest of motion, albeit the very slow motion of rocks in a stream that are borne along and gradually eroded by the action of water coursing over and around them. This arrest, this motionless motion, is effected by an artful juxtaposition of edges, rendered contiguous by the sculptor—even if often invisibly so connected.

Quasha is an edge master extraordinaire, whose gift consists in disclosing the genius of stones to cling to each other at their extremities—at their edges.

2

This sculptor is also a poet, a rare and highly improbable combination. The same person who balances weighty stones also shapes weightless words. In his aerated poetry we witness wisps of edges that act in counterpoint with those that inform the gravity of his stonework. "Let the stones act on you" ("Response Request: Whence What Come," *Verbal Paradise*, 34), he writes, and by this he means act on us both lithically and poetically. The stones act with and by their own dense means, but they can also work their way into language by *l'alchimie du verbe*. Despite the difference in manifest materiality, the acting and the working—the literal *Wirkung*—happens through the edge.

THE EDGE IS WHERE THE ACTION IS. The edge acts at and as the point of impingement, whether of 2 + 1 stones or of n + 1 words. Like stones axially arranged, words work on one another through their edges. Quasha creates axes of concatenated stones just as he finds for words inner threads of sense and rhythm that constitute an axis just as invisible, and just as effective, as that which he realizes with stones. This double edging constitutes him as a biaxial artist.

Axis is always a matter of balance. In poetry the balance is no longer literal, a matter of finding and keeping physical balance (which implicates weight and force). Instead, it is a matter of locating words in a skein of meanings—achieving a delicate balance of significance and structure rather than of material substance and thinghood.

"Meaning arises at the edge of signs,"[3] and this is all the more intensely so in the case of poetic meaning. Quasha embraces Merleau-Ponty's quasi-structuralist thesis when he writes that "There's *a meaning between assertions* the poem can hardly escape" (*Verbal Paradise*, 34). Or else:

> Stand still when you smile at meaning waving your quill.
> *Wonder further!*
>
> Line, circumstance—going straight in bounding the empty.
> Sign on the ledge: *slight alteration in signal wakes across.*
>
> *Would the* un*dead please line* up.
> Nature articulates particulates.
>
> ...*round bird cry situating in the moment that engenders it...*
> Torque potentiates the tongue that conjures.
>
> In the mon*d*ologue the world is only description, strut, strut.
> Everything slants according to the life/death outcome of the present instant.
>
> Discovery makes us—reach out lip first.
> The legible edge strips bare.
>
> ("A Hunt for Defining Gesture Hints the Stroke Ending All Doubt," *Verbal Paradise,* 30).

This poem abounds in edge aspects. "Bounding the empty" is tracing the edge of that which has no distinguishable content. Being "on the ledge" is tantamount to being on the edge. "Articulates" is an action of drawing the limit of something with the sweep of one's arm. "The present instant" is the temporal equivalent of the point-edge, given that the instant is the lower bound of duration.

---

[3] Maurice Merleau-Ponty, "Signs" in his *Signs*, tr. R. McCleary (Evanston: Northwestern University Press, 1964), 41: "this meaning arising at the edge of signs, this immanence of the whole in the parts...."

Other poems of Quasha's show a comparable edge sensitivity, above all the recently composed "preverbs," poems which in stopping short of full-fledged verbs end by giving a subtle intimation of the edges of things named by nouns and noun phrases—in short, a "mon*d*ologue" in which "the world is only description." We are here at the doorstep of phenomenology. Common to such poetry and to classical phenomenological description alike is a shared *liminology*, a preoccupation for limits and thresholds and other varieties of edge. "Yet here we are at the threshold of cutting oneself off along the line" (*Verbal Paradise*, 34).

Another poem, another line: "Still joint. / The line of vision horizons the real, reeling."[4] At work is the close imbrication of edges of diverse descriptions, including joints, lines, horizons, reels. The effect is that of a dense matrix of edges—as thick in its way as is the substance of the stone that Sisyphus rolls up the mountain in repeatedly vain gestures.

The edge that matters most in poetry is the *line*. In composing preverbs, Quasha is preoccupied with the task of putting words onto discrete lines—reeling them into these lines, locating them there before they fly away into the obscure reaches of connotation. That is to say, he is vigilant in his effort to *put them onto the edge constituted by the poetic line.* Such linearity comes to a head in these lines from "Thorough Through & Through":

> Declaring poetic vocation responds to a call to put it all on the line.
> There stones lie with people, words in their sounds lie, lyres lie aligned.
> Otherwise the line is wide open.
> We shift on the ground according to undersensed variables.
>
> (*Verbal Paradise*, 33)

In poetic alignment we find the wordwise equivalent of finding the axial line between precariously balanced stones. An axis, after all, is a line—

[4] From "And Sisyphus a Huge Round Stone Did Reel" (*Verbal Paradise*, 33). In this poem a stone repeatedly rolled upward returns to the base of the mountain—as if to suggest the poet's endlessly repeated efforts to reach the summit of sense, only to fall back again into nonsense, moving in two ways across the edges of signs.

stones lift mind first

Axial Stones #36 with preverb

whether it is a predominantly vertical line as in stone sculpture or a horizontal one as in preverbial poetry.[5] Around the line, in it and as it, we find the edge in which all biaxial art converges.

"Everything flourishes at the edge": these words of Derrida, meant as a claim about Kant's treatment of the *parergon*, hold true for Quasha's artwork.[6] This is work that is finely balanced between the outposts of the line. Just as edge-points strike sparks between ill-fitting stones—much as words are the scintillae of the poem—so the line-edge is the filament that draws out stones and words alike, the former toward the art of physical balance, the latter toward the array of equipoise.

3

The absolute edge: this term came unhesitatingly to Quasha's lips as he talked of his manner of working. He was speaking intensely and almost mystically of that magical moment when an edge is achieved that is, in itself, invisible and intangible.[7] This is an edge absolved of accustomed physical or semiological parameters in space and time. It is the moment of the Event—of the actual occasion of creation, undergone up close in first person. As such, it is not relative to any other experience but sets itself apart as a strictly singular moment, *sans pareil* and *sui generis*. Nor can it be compromised, much less comprised, of anything else: it stands by itself, *selbstgenüg*, self-sufficient, no matter by what processes it has come into being, personal and other-than-personal. It exists in and by itself. In the same conversation Quasha cited Einstein, who said he regretted the

---

[5] "Preverbial" combines and condenses "preverb" and "proverbial."

[6] Jacques Derrida, *The Truth in Painting*, tr. G. Bennington (Chicago: University of Chicago Press, 1987), 151.

[7] This third section draws from a conversation I had with Quasha at Mt. Pocono, Pennsylvania, May 28, 2012. In that discussion, he emphasized that his work proceeds from three basic principles: axiality, liminality, and configuration. In this essay, I am not able to do justice to *configuration*, while focusing on the *edge* aspects of the axial and the liminal. However, a full accounting of his work would have to integrate this latter element so there could be a comprehensive appreciation of his achievement.

connotations of the phrase "theory of relativity," yet couldn't speak of "absolute space and time," as this locution had been pre-empted by Newton in the Scholium to his *Mathematical Principles of Natural Philosophy*.[8]

So regarded, the artwork arises autonomously whatever its heteronomous origins and destination. It is like an *instant* in time—the absolute appearing of temporal process. When Bachelard argued against smooth and spread-out Bergsonian *durée*, he invoked the instant as uniquely able to punctuate the otherwise heavy massive movement of duration.[9] The edge is of comparable necessity in the determination of spatial relations—lest these relations be dissolved in a neutral and indifferent medium, everywhere isotropic and "equably flowing" (Newton). Whether occurring as a threshold or a line, a point or a spot, the edge animates the spaces it acts to delineate.[10] Like the instant, it is an energizing force.

Quasha's extraordinary art takes many forms, none of them indifferently the same as the others, each uniquely realized. In this brief foray into his work, I have singled out his stone sculpture and preverbial poetry. Two unlikely partners, in the end incongruent counterparts: different in internal structuration and medium, they rejoin each other as deeply if tacitly symmetrical attainings. The "link of links"[11] that conjoins them is the *edge*, especially the edge that occurs as *axis*—that is to say, as *line*. Quasha is a biaxial artist whose work is actualized in distinctly linear formats. Each work is liminal in its very axiality, and configured in the *mysterium coniunctionis* of both. The *fil conducteur*, the *Leitfaden*, is throughout the edge.

---

[8] Isaac Newton, *Mathematical Principles of Natural Philosophy*, tr. A. Motte, ed. F. Cajori (Berkeley: University of California Press, 1962), I: 6 (Scholium to the opening Definitions).

[9] See Gaston Bachelard, *L'intuition de l'instant* (Paris: Stock, 1932); English translation, E. Rizo-Patron, *The Intuition of the Instant* (Evanston: Northwestern University Press, 2013).

[10] On the spot, see this line from "Night's Ignition": "The purpose of poetry is to put you back on the spot." (*Verbal Paradise*, 47).

[11] Giordano Bruno, *On the Infinite Universe and Worlds*, tr. D.W. Singer, in D.W. Singer, *Giordano Bruno: His Life and Thought* (New York: Greenwood, 1968), 264.

Edward S. Casey

II
A Matter of Principle On the Edges of Thought[1]

Meanwhile I call from a verge...

George Quasha, "Pre Names the Program to Optimize"[2]

1

Poetry and Principle: are these not incompossible? Isn't a poem utterly unique, a one-time event, both as created and as read? Whereas a principle is, by any usual criterion, *general*: true in many cases, at least all those which the principle superintends, clarifies, structures. In this highly original text (*Poetry in Principle*)—itself a unique event of original thinking—George Quasha opens not just with paradox but with what appears to be an outright contradiction: *poetry/in principle.* A contradiction indeed... unless it turns out that poetry is something more than a discrete happening, and if principle itself proves to be other than unmitigatedly general. It is just this radical re-reading of poetry and principle alike and in relation to each other that Quasha offers to us in this highly condensed trio of essays, each of which bristles with brilliance

---

[1] This essay was written as a forward to George Quasha's *Poetry in Principle: Essays in Poetics*, 2019, which comprises the three essays "Poetry in Principle," "Healing Poetics," and "The Poetics of Thinking"; each had appeared separately online and remains archived there (see bibliography). Page citations in parentheses hereafter to *Poetry in Principle* refer to the 2019 print edition (*Poetry in Principle: Essays in Poetics*, foreword by Edward S. Casey, 2019; hereinafter cited in text parenthetically).

[2] *Things Done for Themselves (preverbs)*, 2015, 21; hereinafter cited in text parenthetically.

and all of which contribute to a radical re-interpretation of poetry and principle alike—and of much else besides.

My earliest memory of Quasha was at a Buddhist retreat in western Massachusetts. He was kneading the backs of anyone willing to let him do so. He was doing so with a special intensity that intrigued as well as puzzled me: was this the time and place for physical therapy? But friends of mine were gladly receiving George's ministrations, and were evidently grateful for them. Little did I know that whatever actual therapeutic effect may then have been happening, something else was at stake. It was a matter of principle.... Just as poetry and principle are thrust together in Quasha's thinking, so the healing of bodies by touch also occurs by way of principle: in both cases, we have to do with what Plato called an "indefinite dyad" (*ahoristos dyas*): like and unlike, odd and even, same and different.

2

We encounter this dyad first of all in what Quasha calls "healing poetics." These two words themselves are oxymoronic when put together: how can healing—which has to do with concrete issues of health and well-being—relate to poetics, which spells out the infrastructure of poetic discourse and appears to have nothing to do with lived bodies and their health? And yet Quasha, against all odds, demonstrates that subtending both of these domains is the axial principle, which "understands bodymind phenomena as self-regulating and self-organizing." Derived from Quasha's long-time immersion in t'ai chi—where what matters is refusing to combat the other directly—Quasha maintains that the same axial principle, properly inflected, is also operative in quite various arts, including poetry, drawing and painting, music, and sculpture. In each case, from healing to sculpting, the axiality is at work in a process of "transitive mirroring" in which the artist or healer refuses to stop at the surface of the art work or the skin of the other, instead going *through* the surface to the other side. Quasha invokes the scene in Cocteau's *Orphée* in which Orpheus is shown "passing through his 'reflection' to its otherwhere." In contrast with Lacan's mirror stage—in which the child is arrested at the surface of the mirror and identifies with a literally superficial image—here the artist and the healer alike eschew the temptation to collapse into what is literally seen or touched, and instead allow themselves to merge with the larger environment in an action of *ecoproprioception* in which one's self-perception is "non-separate from environment."

But still: what can hands-on bodywork have to do with hands-off poetry? *Everything*—understood at the right level. The ingredient principle adumbrates this level in the guise of an invisible axis around which circulate apparent incompatibilities that the axis itself, invisible and intangible as such, renders compatible and mutually reinforcing. When Quasha as bodyworker helps himself and others to find their invisible corporeal core, or when he puts together groups of stones by finding the exactly right if precarious level of balance that allows each group to stand on its own, the operative principle effects a *co-inherence* not just between discrete stones or within disparate human bodies but between the two apparently unrelated circumstances themselves. Bodies and stones—as well as poetic words and theatrical performances—coil around the same axis.[3]

A principle such as the axial principle, then, does not just adjudicate between competing instances and apparent counter-instances but actively *renders compossible* what is presented as incompatible or unrelated to begin with. A principle does not order from above as on a classical metaphysical model—e.g., as in the "Synthetic Principles of Pure Understanding" in Kant's *Critique of Pure Reason*[4]—but renders apparent dis- or un-order as ordered from within. Just as reading a dense poem

---

[3] See *Axial Stones: An Art of Precarious Balance.* Note that the Prologue to this volume already discusses the principles of "open axis," "liminality," and "configuration."

[4] See *Critique of Pure Reason B197-98/A158–59.* There Kant remarks: "That there should be principles at all is entirely due to the pure understanding. For not only is it the faculty of rules with regard to that which happens, but [pure understanding] is itself the source of principles according to which everything (that can become an object to us) is necessarily subject to rules." (Kant, *Critique of Pure Reason,* tr. Max Muller, ed. Marcus Weigelt [Penguin, 2007], 189). Key here is the idea of "pure understanding," which underlies all human knowledge and which operates by its own *a priori* principles.

for the first time baffles and intrigues the reader, so it yields to an immanent sense-making order upon successive readings.[5]

In these various ways, Quasha leads us not just to a particular principle but to *the working principle of principle itself.* Thanks to this, what is experienced as initially disjunctive and as belonging to distinctly different domains (e.g., human body/poetic text/pile of stones/vigorous brushstrokes as in Quasha's axial drawings) is recognized as immanently intertangled. This is not a matter of identifying a new and different domain—another genus for these various species, as it were—but of showing how a tacit reticular structure holds together these divergent phenomena *from below* (*von unten*: in Karl Jaspers' term) rather than assembling them from above or from without. This is not a formal structure but a *dimension of sameness that harbors and holds difference as a constitutive feature*. As Heidegger maintains in "Identity and Difference," sameness *requires* difference if it is to be as generous and receptive as human experience attests—in contrast with identity, which excludes difference by its very exclusivity. Likewise, a Quashian principle thrives on difference even as it collects widely divergent phenomena in the loose sameness of the Indra's net it casts. "Identity is the play of sames," he writes in one of his recent preverbs,[6] meaning that identity is a function of sameness rather than the other way around as the metaphysics of presence in the West would have it.

George Quasha is a past master of detecting differences that share a principled sameness. This is all the more impressive as he takes us to truly *eidetic* differences that make a difference and are not merely analytic or scholastic. A pertinent case in point is the difference between a principle and a concept. A concept, literally 'seizing together', is an idea that draws together related differences and arranges theses end-to-end in a single exhaustive spectrum. A concept orders *down* (down

[5] *Poetry in Principle* starts from Quasha's own early draw to poetry which he admits he did not grasp at first—whether that of Eliot, Stevens or Mac Low—but which he came to realize manifested an inherent *Regelmässigkeit* [regularity, persistence] that was always there even if it was initially as invisible as it was inaudible.

[6] From "Ending Up On the Very Spot" in *Things Done for Themselves*, 55.

from the concept itself) and orders *out*—out into one homogeneous experiential field. It is a controlling term, and leaves little room for the kind of creative difference on which poetry and all the arts, as well as healing regarded as a non-reiterative mirroring practice, thrive. The aim in conceptual analysis is clarity and distinctness—the two criteria of epistemically valid ideas for Descartes and much of modern Western thought. Whereas the effect of principles in the amplified sense proposed by Quasha is to open up whole *fields* of meaning, fields whose content is characterized by "heterogeneous multiplicity" (Bergson) and whose layout is that of "smooth space" (Deleuze and Guattari). Quashian principles are at once heterogeneous and smooth.

A field for Quasha is an expansive scene in which difference triumphs over identity in the generation of a vital sense of the same. Instead of down and out being the primary vectors, the dimensions that matter come from *underneath* and ramify *across* eidetic differences, linking them in a loose assemblage of diverse directions.

3

So far I have been emphasizing the role of principle at stake in *Poetry in Principle*. This role must be set apart from that of deductive and metaphysical "principles" that are held to organize experience from above—an "above" that is variously labeled as "transcendental" or "metaphysical" with an eye to the attainment of certainty and knowledge down below under the supervision of these same principles. But principles signify not abstractions but concretions—the concretions of immersion in matter, whether this be the materiality of the lived body, the layout of an environment, or of stones assembled on top of each other, or the sublime matter of the poetic text.

In contrast with the *lumen naturale* of concepts and categories, Quasha takes us into the heart of epistemic darkness by arguing that ecoproprioception delivers to us something quite different from facts or knowledge or theory: it offers to us the felt truth of experience as it occurs in the realm of bodily awareness and poetic sensibility. This truth is a material truth; it is the truth of (the) matter. This is a truth that emerges only when principle is ingredient in matter itself, whether that of the live body in the process of being healed, the "dead" lithic matter of juxtaposed stones, or the weightless matter of the poetic text. Just as Kant's exclusive emphasis on the formal *a priori* structures of knowledge gave way to the exploration of a properly material *a priori* in the work of Scheler, Ingarden, and Dufrenne,[7] so Quasha has replaced a formal poetics of the poem and a medical ethics of healing with a material poetics of immanent, ecoproprioceptive meaning or "felt sense" (in Gendlin's term)[8] that animates all such otherwise heterogeneous domains. And other domains as well—thanks to the active ingredience of the various principles that make possible the unholy alliances to which Quasha points us in *Poetry in Principle*. All of this is a matter of principle indeed, for it exhibits the material immanence of principles themselves in diversely disposed realms of experience.

This is so despite the fact that these principles are (in Quasha's provocative phrase) "thinking principles." They are principles that ingress into matter and make it accessible from within–as poetry, sculpture, healing, philosophy.[9] But this can happen only if we are dealing with principles "behind thinking, but also principles engaged in thinking—principles themselves seeming to think independently of us" (93). Principles, in other words, link thinking and specific engagements in art and healing; they are the *metaxu* of otherwise disparate domains, their connective tissue.

At the level of experience, the efficacy of principles is due to the working of ecoproprioception, defined as "self experienced as other–as lived environment." One basic way this happens is through the lived body

[7] Phenomenologists Max Scheler (1874-1928), Roman Ingarden (1893-1970), and Mikel Dufrenne (1910-1995).

[8] Philosopher and psychotherapist Eugene T. Gendlin (1926-2017) whose work in "philosophy of the implicit" and "Focusing" Quasha acknowledges as an influence.

[9] Philosophy has its own poetics, a "poetics of thinking" which, Quasha notes, "makes new thinking possible and may even discover new dimensions of the thinkable, beyond all categories."

regarded as "the knowing body" (*le corps connaissant* in Merleau-Ponty's phrase). Quasha would prefer to say "the thinking body." For the body, as ecoproprioceptive, is said to be a body that "can think outside itself–[it is a] self thinking afield.... It can think something approaching *field mindfulness*" (80, his italics). We are here taking mind out of body–not to put it in a separate place such as the brain or a separate substantial container such as *res cogitans* provides–but in order to resituate it in field phenomena such as the natural environment, the poetic text, the body-to-be-healed. The binaries of mind vs. body, or self vs. other, are replaced with a single spatio-temporal expanse in which I cannot ultimately distinguish myself from the field and its contents. It is a matter of a liminal space and time whose limits are boundaries rather than borders, thresholds rather than walls.[10] In regard to art and philosophy alike, "the work itself [is] *limen*" (111)—where *limen* is taken as "a sensory threshold, hence barely perceptible" (112).

Into such space I am invited to enter—to *participate.*[11] The participation is not only by way of ritual process, as in *participation mystique*, but by way of an expanded mind that, attaining mindfulness, engages matter. And this means in turn to engage principle. For we are here in a generous loop whose nodal points include thinking, principle, matter, mind, mindfulness, and ecoproprioception. It would be a mistake—a mistake of principle—to try to discern any strict hierarchy in this set of six terms, just as it would be mistaken to limit the list itself (which also includes poetics, healing, text, language, theater, etc.). Quasha is taking us far afield. But that is just the point. We must travel far north to understand more discerningly what is happening down south, go way

[10] As Quasha writes with characteristic force and flair, "There's an intrinsic liminality here between text and environment, page-writing as limen between internal language-music and active exterior world—page-space refocusing (self) awareness through surround sound/space/linguality. Field mindfulness, proprioceptive field thinking...," 83.

[11] "This special use of *participate* (not followed by 'in') extends the post-Durkheim/Lévy-Bruhl term of Owen Barfield—for experiencing phenomena without separating subject and object—to include a *willing liminality*, a standing between apparent contraries in order to openly inquire...," 92.

east to determine what's up in the west. In this journey, there's no other way to go except every which way—if we are to go anywhere other than stay at the dead center of literal fact and diremptive dyads.... We must go to the edge....

4

George Quasha, in the liminal text that is *Poetry in Principle*, takes us to the edge: not just to the edge of his own evolving thinking about art and healing practices but to the edge of thinking itself. This edge takes place most specifically as *language*, which can be considered the edge of thought appearing in words, whether on a printed page of poetry or in a theatrical production. The latter emerges as paradigmatic once it is considered as "theater of more"—giving us more than we had ever expected, not just more spectacle, but more of the non-literal truth of things and events, and ultimately more of ourselves in the wake of seeing a theatrical performance such as a Noh production. Theater takes place literally as a liminal space between performers and audience—a very special kind of moving edge in which the audience is invited to participate via a common medium of language. "Language," writes Quasha, "holds the center as the very possibility of saying, not necessarily, of course, with words, but also with movement, gesture, sound—and, at least since Artaud, theatre has remembered itself as a language of more than words."[12] As "living language [speaking] for itself," a theatrical performance is the incarnation of "theater thinking" (95).

Despite the peculiar power of theatrical language to incarnate spatial and temporal edges, *the edge of edges is principle itself*, which frames the essay as a whole and to which Quasha fittingly returns in the final pages. "That's the starting point in this inquiry into principle; the realization that *a principle shows itself in the language by which it is thought*. And that language has what should be recognized as a *poetics*" (86).

---

[12] He continues: "Gesture can speak as unambiguously or as ambiguously as words, and the meaning-continuum of sound and gesture is as intensive and extensive as words, semantics, syntax, rhetoric," 102.

Beyond theater—if there is any such beyond—there is the principled work of principle itself. This work cannot be defined as such: "A principle can never be defined definitively, because any given definition is itself only a manifestation of the principle itself, merely appearing to be outside it" (105).[13]

In the end, there are three principles at work in art and healing: axial, liminal, and configurative: "These three terms comprise both a complex principle, as I see it in its tripartite appearance, and a possible (but not necessary) sequence in the interrelated way that the principle unfolds in experience. They also embody three ultimately inseparable aspects of a commitment to principle in art" (107). Or let us put it this way: the three principles are covalent edges of a basic commitment to principle in art. This is suggested by Quasha's claim that "a true manifestation of principle, the way I mean it here, is a singularity" (108). For the ultimate singularity is edge itself, which is responsible for presenting a thing, person, or event as uniquely itself—as we witness in the case of distinctive profiles of many kinds.

To move to edge is in keeping with Quasha's own thinking. In the penultimate sentence of his ever-exfoliating book, he says expressly that "principle thinking" in "its search for a possible poetics, is always turning and situating itself within its axis, always playing itself out at the edge, and always configuring itself and the reality before it" (116). Indeed, what is an axis but an interior edge around which various phenomena circulate, what is a *limen* but the edge of a threshold, and what is configuration but the articulation of the edges of particular things

[13] Nevertheless, Quasha does attempt, with some misgiving, to define principle: "Provisionally I would say principle is the basic or essential element determining the evident functioning of particular natural phenomena, mechanical processes, or art emergence," 106. I am myself wary of the language of "basic" and "essential element" since this gives to principle the kind of epistemic and/or metaphysical priority that Quasha's own deployment of principle dispenses with. As he says himself, "the root principle is open," 106.

and events? Edge is at stake throughout. As Quasha has said elsewhere, "in the self-organizing reality everything is always on edge. There is only edge."[14]

This last claim holds especially for what I like to call "thinking on the edge." Modeled on Dogen's schema of *hi-shiryó*, this is the path from which reflective thinking emerges.[15] It is striking that Quasha is himself concerned with "rethinking 'reflection' not as static or repetitive but rather as a journey out of stasis" (53)."[16] For him, the ultimate act of reflection is that of thinking (in terms of) principles. Such thinking is a reflecting that leads from the edges evident in ecoproprioception to those characterizing poetic principles–indeed, to the entire enterprise of "principle thinking." All such principles and precisely such thinking, along with the experiential matters to which they give access, are edge phenomena—"periphenomena," as I prefer to call them. When we approach principled thinking, we do so by means of the edges of thought itself, and it is these very edges that give access to the materialities of the to-be-healed body, the poetic text, barely balanced stones, and theatrical performances. It is all a matter of principle in the edge-worlds to which George Quasha gives us such ample access in the transformational text that lies before you in the three essays of *Poetry in Principle*. Open it, take in its splendors, and learn from it–learn how to find the place of principled thinking in creative endeavors of every imaginable sort.

---

[14] George Quasha, email to author (January 11, 2016).

[15] On *hi-shiryó*, see Edward S. Casey, *The World on Edge* (Bloomington: Indiana University Press, 2017), Afterward/Forward: "Thinking Edges, Edges of Thinking," esp. 362-64.

[16] Quasha adds that a renewed sense of reflection "can open [in such] a way that the discipline of poiesis/poetics is relevant to healing, and, on the mirror principle, vice versa," 53—and, as he shows subsequently, relevant also to the material textuality of poetry and theater.

Robert Kelly

Hearing Quasha's *Preverbs:* A Note

Anyone who has had the privilege of hearing George Quasha read from his *preverbs* will know that every one of the thousands of lines in that immense and still-growing text wants to be read, spoken, all by itself. A line speaks, and falls silent.

Those who know the text only from the page may allow their disobedient eyes, those creatures of habit, to read on and on, nimbly leaping the space between one line and the next as if it weren't there, as if the text had been put on the page by some mad printer with a terribly short attention span. The reader must learn to resist this assumption, must take seriously what the page shows, those eloquent gaps betwixt and between those potent lines.

One evening we were all sitting around, and George read some of the latest communiques from the great campaign of the *preverbs.* As he read—and this all who have heard his public readings will remember—at each line his hand (the one not holding the page) would gesture, clearly, forcefully, explainingly, towards his hearers. And after every single line he would look up at us in front of him, as if making sure the line had come all the way over to us.

It was a moving experience, watching the quiet urgency with which each line was sent our way. Moving, yes, but also hauntingly reminiscent of something else. It was hours later, back home, as I drifted towards sleep in dark comfort, that I remembered what it was Quasha's reading had nudged me to recall:

In a French movie, you know the one, the young man stands before the mirror, staring into it, and repeating over and over again his own name: Antoine Doinel, Antoine Doinel, Antoine Doinel until his name becomes only sounds. (François Truffaut's *Stolen Kisses* [*Baisers volés*], 1968.) And there I saw George, speaking intently each syllable of his own immense name, for our true name in eternity is all we have spoken. And there he was, gazing into the glass of the Other, us, sitting there.

In turn, that memory led me to understand Quasha's lines as an interminable (I hope) series of self-interrogations—statements that rise from the depths of language and provoke him into speech: statements he can only verify by saying them into the silence, then waiting for what happens next. What speaks next. So when I look for an 'argument' as poets used to call the theme or plot of the poem to come, I reproach myself for cowardice, for looking for a logic when I am given so freely the wild cry of an animal seeking its own nature by its cries. The wolf howls to find itself.

So it seemed to me, Quasha on the basic human quest to know the self, using the poet's road (method means following a road): knowing the self by saying—and in that saying, the Other is implicitly, inescapably, invoked. *Hieros gamos*, the sacred marriage, happens when the self truly says itself, boldly, facing the other. And so it was that late evening, Quasha's eyes seeking himself in the mirror of his listeners, generously, firmly, one sentence at a time. And letting the silence sing between each cry, letting the echo swoon away.

We come away from hearing a good poet read reinforced with a basic awareness, one so simple and so profound that it eludes most schoolmasters and literary critics—silence is the essence of poetry, silence that shapes the poet's utterances and shapes simultaneously our reception of them, silence parceling out the goods of speech, silence turning the on-and-on of prose into a discrete music, shaping the pitch, the tone, the feeling of the event, line by line, gap by gap. *Ginnungagap*, the Old Norse word for the primal void in and from which the world was made.

14 October 2018

Cover of Ainu Dreams *(1999)*

Kimberly Lyons

A Penchant for Reporting the Liminal[1]

a massive contact lens
iridescent
and collecting dew along the base

—this is a thing so
transparently fragile
I'm scared stiff I'll break it [...]

(*Ainu Dreams,* "Sitting on Thin Glass")[2]

These opening lines from a poem embodying a Japanese artist's dream characterize the elusive and playful universe of oneiric possibilities engaged in *Ainu Dreams* (1999), a set of eighty poems George Quasha began writing in 1994 in collaboration with Chie Hasegawa (aka buun and now, Chie Hammons). *Ainu Dreams* conveys a pictorial, enigmatic magic and flexible dimensionality of consciousness that remain a durably attracting spiritual encounter. My exploration here, focusing in part on the book's linkage to Quasha's subsequent writing projects, has reconnected me with that initial exhilarating reading and "takes me back/ to the unrecallable place" (*AD,* 108).

This set of poems offers many valences, multiple entrances into a specialized universe of enigmatic conditions and quixotic encounters. The singular objects and instruments that Hasegawa dreams, which in part constitute the substance of these poems, could themselves be a focus of

[1] The title cites a phrase from George Quasha and Charles Stein, "Publishing Blanchot in America: A Metapoetic View," in Maurice Blanchot, *The Station Hill Blanchot Reader,* ed. George Quasha, in collaboration with Charles Stein (Barrytown: Station Hill Press, 1995), 512; hereinafter cited in text parenthetically.

[2] George Quasha (with Chie Hasegawa), *Ainu Dreams,* 1999, 101; hereinafter cited in text parenthetically.

examination—as would any individual states of consciousness emerging in funny and instructive ways.

One path of reading through the poems in this volume is to trace possible traditional associations (such as Buddhist, Japanese, Western Hermetic, even shamanic) including animal creatures (a blue dragon, dragon fly look-alikes, a white dog, a wolf and an elephant, a red bird, light baby bees, a huge white bear, a white retriever, and peacocks), which the Japanese dreamer encounters, along with various ancestor presences, in often hilariously related episodes. These entities, sometimes seeming like guardians, herald an otherness of being, with provocative ritual gestures, to anyone entering the Hasegawa/Quasha dream realm.

What I find most compelling is the plasticity of the reality-frames that the poems invoke. A fantastic malleability of self and radical shape-shifting rupture the time-space continuum, accomplished in minute, subtle gestures that transfigure states of being: a "very particular body movement/which can only be done in a certain state" (*AD,* 21). Feeling becomes aura: "the poet/became a soft lavender,/The shape of the body was unchanged but the rest was color,/pure pervasive lavender" (*AD,* 46). An often simple diction succinctly conveys the curious action as it happens: "I myself am a bird"; "out came two trans/parent wings"; "autumn leaves came out of my mouth"; "I am an apple"; "We are roses." (*AD,* 17, 19, 32, 35, 36).

The trippy acrobatic change-ups unexpectedly suggest a spiritual equanimity; and a dream traveler's surprise as if landing on the other end of a wormhole—"I accidentally found an invisible door, and lo!/ It lifted right out of the front of my body" [*AD,* 68])—encourages the reader to align with a transportive narrative: "existable/residues" progress to "still more/reaching dimensions" (*AD,* 25). An elasticity of being strengthens through the cognitive dynamics of reading. Such dynamics raise questions. Can engaged reading of poetry unleash cognitive capacities and stored dream communiqués, which retracing neural pathways re-ignites? Do poetry's compressed forms interact with mental "storage" to concentrate concepts and pictures in swift sequence that imprints alogical imaginings?

After one reading of *Ainu Dreams*, I dreamt of a cheetah wandering through the dream span. The next night, again, a cheetah passed by with a penetrating glance. (Ten minutes after I write these words, an actual mouse trundles into the room.) Quasha has said that after reading the poems monthly to a group of artists, poets, and musicians, they often reported excited dreaming; indeed, the poet Jackson Mac Low told Quasha that he kept *Ainu Dreams* by his bed to read, before sleeping, for the impact it had on his dreams. And Quasha writes that, in the composition of the poems, he and Hasegawa discovered just such interactions:

> The torque of telling has a quality of transport, to "a land" of its own dimension, implying a language specific to another dimension, to which poetry is liminal. The poem is aroused transversely by the listening, is moved to mind the gap. (*AD,* 134)

A probable objective of any poem is to come fully into being. Such effort extends radially, engaged causally in all directions, with apparent impact on surroundings. Among the *Ainu Dreams* trajectories is one tracing an ineffable dream intelligence as it demonstrates the capacity of language to torque its own materiality. In the graphic dream-sphere space of the poems, the sign dematerializes, but not as a deconstruction; rather, by a synesthetic further manifestation within a layer of the possible: "Translation before my eyes/into many, many luminous spots" (*AD,* 32). Surfaces resize into porous textures, as in "latticing/its own life, turning into sounds" (*AD*, 19) and "the green glow in the ground calling to the surface" (*AD,* 118). "A word surfaces/Oki Oki" (*AD,* 111) suggests dreamed amplification of a phrase that mirrors the emergence of word into written text. "The words themselves glow,/expand" (*AD,* 116).

Ainu Dreams enacts a metaphysic we may have encountered in historical and contemporary trance texts, in which it is proposed that perceived spatiality and constructions of reality ("old whatevers" [*AD,* 78]) are informed and limited by intentions and emotion. In *The Mystical Languages of Unsaying,* Michael Sells' exploration of apophatic discourses, he discusses the Sufi mystic Ibn Arabi's concept of "the error of binding [*taquid*]." The *binding* of consciousness to naming's ontological categories narrows our capacity to perceive a larger cosmic reality. The permeability of frameworks in *Ainu Dreams* playfully challenges this tendency.

There is yet another perspective offered by *Ainu Dreams.* I would suggest that the dyadic project, 1994-1999, with Hasegawa as dreamer/narrator and indeed co-editor where Quasha serves as scribe, poet, and co-editor, contributed to the onset in 2000 of the *preverbs* project. This approach might indicate how one dimension of Quasha's poetics prefigures a further development and repeats an earlier history as well, going all the way back to the 1960s.

Quasha has noted in various statements of poetics that prior to the onset of *preverbs* he had written poems he originally called *torsional,* which in later work evolved into *axial.* The former grew out of his engagement with the work of William Blake, informed simultaneously by discoveries he made in D'Arcy Wentworth Thompsons's *On Growth and Form* (1917). First signs of what would become *axial/preverbial* work showed up, he reports, in writing from dreams in 1967, which became the "Proverbs of Soma" (part of the extended poetic sequence "Of a Woman the Earth Bore to Keep").[3] Composed in his mid-twenties while working on the essay, "Orc as a Fiery Paradigm of Poetic Torsion,"[4] Quasha applied Thompson's morphological analysis of the torsional growth of vines to a reading of Blake's figure of Orc as revolutionary action in *America a Prophecy* (1793). The paradigm of poetic torsion stands behind an early series of Quasha's "torsion poems"[5] and

---

[3] *Stony Brook Journal 1/2,* 1968. Quasha's own writing from dreams remained an important part of his work at least throughout the 1970s, as in the "Somaoneirika" series (*An Active Anthology,* edited by George Quasha with Susan Quasha, Fremont, MI: Sumac Press, 1974). Dreams played importantly in his main series of the 1970s, *Somapoetics* (Vol. I, Sumac Press, 1973).

[4] *Blake's Visionary Forms Dramatic,* edited by David V. Erdman and John T. Grant. Princeton: 1970. Quasha's essay is available online at academia.edu.

[5] Torsion poems include "The Weight of the Matter or Where It Is Pulling" and "Homage to What I Hear Is So" written in 1969 and published in *Open Poetry: Four Anthologies of Expanded Poems,* eds. Ronald Gross and George Quasha, with Emmett Williams, John Robert Colombo and Walter Lowenfels (New York: Simon & Schuster, 1973), 164-169.

later morphs into axial poetics in poems over many years and eventually into *preverbs*.

I would suggest that *Ainu Dreams* picked up one strand of that earlier dream sourcing, the origin of which came in parallel to biological processes and Blakean "poetic prophecy." Other strands embodying and reporting on instances of radical change indicate that Quasha underwent some sort of initiation, one that eventually brought him to the threshold of specific modalities at work in *preverbs*. Tracing a linkage from the torsional syntax poems, connected to the thinking in the Orc essay and various other writings, we can see a progression in his work that is in fact aligned with Thompson's concept of spiral development (in horns and vines).

The twisting and turning in the growth of a vine, or its slower parallel in the formation of horns and antlers, becomes a principle of syntax in the torsion poems related in principle to Blake's *America a Prophecy*. Intensively reading Blake for so many years Quasha developed a practice with a principle of torsional change—a malleability of language mind and radical receptivity that challenged poetic convention. This challenge comes not necessarily from Orc-like youthful breaking away or a modernist insistence on the "new," nor out of disrespect for traditional literary streams and their poetic forms; rather, it comes as a positive quest, in sympathy with, as Quasha wrote in the torsion essay, Blake's "expansion by prosodic and structural unfettering." The actual *collaborative* process of *Ainu Dreams* was itself a spiraled torsion in which the poet's process was a vine-like growth by encountering the language and experience of another and the extreme otherness of dream.

Here I'm thinking about the sessions of Hasegawa's actively speaking the dream aloud and Quasha's listening practice that on the spot "translated" and worked her Japanese English into the fabric of a poem. He writes in "A Word Before," prefatory to *Ainu Dreams*:

> I have written the poems in active collaboration with the dreamer, who was most often physically present during some part of the writing process and exerted a continuous, sharp and uncompromising corrective force upon composition. The poems are deeply

> faithful to the dreams and preserve their actual content, and even in various ways the language of the dreamer, as possible. At the same time, *Ainu Dreams* is a work inside poetry and develops according to the inner necessity of the poem itself and by a *meta-poetic* principle: that each poem embodies an originary poetics, unique to its own possibility. (*AD,* 12)

The active listening to the uniqueness of the dream reinforces a principle of "each poem embodies an originary poetics"—a principle that will become the heart of *preverbs* where this could be said of each line. Quasha continues:

> For my part I have found in this work a new confirmation of my lifelong view of the poem as having its source *outside* the known boundaries of personal reality, even when the poem seems most personal. I understand the poet's role as maintaining a discipline of listening to the source, here situated at once in the dream and in emerging language. Poetry is first of all *speaking with listening*—a peculiar state that is somehow self-optimizing, somehow self-awakening. (*AD,* 12)

It's possible to see how that listening intensified into a kind of new, or newly sharpened, reception instrumental to *preverbs* composition. In "a note on preverbs and axial poetics," published on Jerome Rothenberg's blog "Poems and Poetics" Quasha discusses how in *preverbs*

> [t]he projective force, beyond the line (or syntactic unit), is not forward but *radial,* and of course highly variable in reading [...]. This includes a "poetics of service"; how we serve by *listening* [...]."[6]

I can't help wondering if the composition of *Ainu Dreams,* in part written by listening intensely to a speaker, may have contributed to Quasha's

---

[6] poemsandpoetics.blogspot.com. A related project that employs a different kind of listening is Quasha's ongoing video portraits comprising the separate series, *art is, poetry is,* and *music is* in which hundreds of artists, poets and musicians from many countries respond in singular videotaped portraits to the Quasha's request to say what it—art/poetry/music—*is*: art-is-international.org.

subsequent non-dream-centered work, considering his observation in "Pre Gloss," prefatory to *Glossodelia Attract* (2015):

> In my ear it implies that intense speaking can spontaneously reveal the unknown. Then it *attracts* the mind to further (un)knowing. As psychotropic language vehicle, preverbs can reorient the mind by shifting conceptions of what language is. (xi)

Based on my sense of the voice(s) and address across the *preverbs* I hear a specifically female voice/presence/daimon transmission—a *within*, *from*, or *to* that comes in fact between poet and text. As the *preverb* pronounces within the auditor's listening field, an afterthought inscribes a vanishing "she" whose identity is doubted and reengaged in its elusive flickerings: "Also feeling female the language lets me in another layer to do her waiting./I'm only responsible for what I can't control."[7] Perhaps the dynamic of *Ainu Dreams*' composition allowed the poet to develop a special hearing:

> *It's* muse *when you've heard it from the beginning and still can't recall.*
>
> (*The Daimon of the Moment*, 14)

Quasha himself has engaged with such questions of source, particularly in Thomas Fink's 2016 interview with him for *Jacket2*: "They [preverbs] have the strange quality of seeming both mine and wholly other."[8] Any over-concretization of source comes into question: "Preverbs seem to want to stay within possible syntactic bounds (inviting thought to try them on), which they violate, perhaps becoming paratactic, through internal multiplicity" (10). Further elaboration widens the possibilities of what is speaking and who is listening:

> Preverbs also stand at the lintel of *self and other* and listen in on the ongoing conversation. In that focus they perform a

---

[7] *The Daimon of the Moment (preverbs)*, 2015, 16.

[8] George Quasha and Thomas Fink, "'Awareness inside Language': On George Quasha's Preverbs," www.Jacket2.org (13 May 2016), see below 158.

> sort of kledomantic gathering of stray language according to a singularity-centered principle of organization.[9]

He characterizes a process of reception:

> I could say I "receive" [the lines of preverbs] but that would imply a sender, which I can't verify or know, even though in certain moments and moods it definitely feels like they're coming from elsewhere. [. . . .] From the beginning preverbs have come mostly preformed and performative in the ear-mind. I write them in a notebook I carry with me everywhere, ever ready to write because I have about thirty seconds before they recede into the noesphere, back to the wild. ("Awareness Inside Language," 158)

This interest in the poem's origin and the degree to which it is "received" is an ancient one, and the relation to what is given in dreams is always relevant. In addition to the "mystical" focus on dreams, there is a social one as well, and it's strongly in evidence in the Hudson Valley where the Quashas and Chie Hasegawa have lived for many years. I lived there when I studied at Bard College and still return often, and I experienced firsthand the longstanding interest among the poets in dreamwork. Robert Kelly, a poet in conversation with the Quashas since the early 1970s (thanks to him Quasha taught as visiting professor at Bard in '75), outlines in his own "An Experimental Program for Dream Research" an intention to "investigate the dream reports of a chosen community."[10] The experiment to track group dream data came to realization with the project *The Annandale Dream Gazette,* an online archive that now includes several hundred entries of dream transcripts written by poets.[11] Charles Stein, a poet collaborating with Quasha since the early 1970s, who is mentioned in the preface to *Ainu Dreams* as being close to the dream project, has remarked in conversation with me that

---

[9] *Verbal Paradise (preverbs)*, 2011, x.

[10] *A Voice Full of Cities: The Collected Essays of Robert Kelly,* edited by Pierre Joris and Peter Cockelbergh (New York: Contra Mundum Press, 2014), 364.

[11] Annandale Dream Gazette (available online).

he imagines an "Other Barrytown," a parallel dream community whose geography aligns with, diverges from, and mirrors the actual Barrytown (where he and the Quashas live).[12] And we can be sure that sites of that other town surface elusively in *Ainu Dreams.*

Other significant forces in Quasha's work dovetailed with the creation of *Ainu Dreams* and subsequently contributed to the start of *preverbs.* An intense period of visual art activities, specifically his axial stone works and a new phase of his axial drawings—eventually presented in *Axial Stones: An Art of Precarious Balance* (2006)—came into focus in the *Ainu Dreams* years. At the beginning of the *Ainu Dreams* process, too, Quasha was still deeply immersed in editing with Charles Stein, and launching with Susan Quasha, Station Hill Press's important collection of Maurice Blanchot's writing, *The Station Hill Blanchot Reader* (1995). In the afterword to *Ainu Dreams,* he quotes Blanchot in a way that affirms the importance of the latter's thought in realizing that the very act of writing is transformative story, or that story in this special sense is performative writing:

> The tale (*récit*) is not the narration of an event, but that event itself, the approach to that event, the place where that event is made to happen—an event which is yet to come and through whose power of attraction the tale can hope to come into being too. (*AD,* 132)

Writing as locus of originary event is manifest in the narrative unfolding in the poem "I Get Reversed":

Try not to get confused or lost:

Which is inside,
which is outside.
I start peeling
from the sexual part
like undressing, folding back
the inside out, slowly.

Where is my center now?

(*AD*, 20)

---

[12] Charles Stein in Conversation with Author (Barrytown, NY, 2015).

The coming "into being" that Blanchot writes of is imagined by Hasegawa/Quasha—or, as it were, the dream—as a membranous brain/vagina/text that is both inside and outside and which alters our concepts of the linearity and purposes of narration. "What's it like to be inside a knot?" (*AD,* 37). As in all of the poems in this book, this question in "I Get Reversed" compels us to reconceive the certainties of surfaces and planes of reality. "This is the only possible way to get there" (*AD,* 21). The split-open vermillion pomegranate poised on the cover of *Ainu Dreams* brings to mind an extreme parallel in Salvador Dali's painting, *The Dream Caused by the Flight of a Bee Around a Pomegranate*: a pomegranate flung forward arcs out of painterly space into the realm where the poem in all its multispherical possibility is spoken, heard, written, and read.

The *Ainu Dreams* project, or the alternative realities it embodies, may have contributed as well to the further creative work of Hasegawa. For example, her handmade book object *Liberalia,* from 2000,[13] presents earthily tinted open-page spreads with a smaller, narrower inset of feathered pages, darkened as though burnt. The inset appears to serve as a labial doorway into the book's spine. I am inclined to read that entrance as akin to the liminality she so fully explored in the dream reports leading to *Ainu Dreams.* (Hasegawa has gone on to collaborate with her husband the artist, David Hammons, and seems to be able to extend a solitary imagination into dyadic art).

Collaboration or what Quasha calls "coperformative engagement" has complexly evolved since *Ainu Dreams* and the subsequent published books of the *preverbs*. Since October 2018, he has collaborated with Susan Quasha on sixteen series, each comprising thirty-four preverb poems and photographs, of which six have been published online: *Hilaritas Sublime, Genius Foci, Hearing Other, Dowsing Axis, Surface Retention,* and *View of the Sleeping Dragon.*[14]

---

[13] Chie Hasegawa, "Liberalia," in *One of a Kind: Unique Artist's Books* (New York: AC Books, 2013), 59.

[14] These are all available online (see bibliography below). Previous to his collaboration with Susan Quasha's photographs he worked in a related way with

Artist and book designer Susan Quasha's photographs appear in *Winter Music* (2014), a collaborative book that brought together her work with a poem by Robert Kelly.[15] Characterized by images of resplendent deep color as well as austere tonalities of black and textured organic elements of sky, trees, gravel, leaves as well as found ephemera such as netting, torn detritus, and close-up swelling biological images, these photographs often swerve away from legibility or conventional framing. The elements both hugely spill outwards and show up as magnified minutiae, eluding comfortable object/subject orientation or easy referentiality or naming. For all the nearly abstract and degraded textures in much of her work, they are undeniably sensuous and ecstatic.

The later charged conversation with *preverbs* in all their anomalous and image-subverting iconoclasm is fascinating and endlessly provocative to a reader. The collaborative process is described in *Hilaritas Sublime* (2020) as follows.

> Our practice is basically that she sends me a photo of her choosing more or less daily, without discussing it with me. Her photographs may have been made at any previous point in time or the same day she chooses it for our work. Usually in the evening when I tend to do this kind of work, I open the photograph for the first time on one computer screen while I do the final composition on another screen. I work with lines (preverbs) that have either been written previously (usually earlier the same day, but not exclusively) or that come new in variable relation to the presence of the image; the new lines usually exceed those already in my notebook. There are no rules about how much preverbs respond directly or indirectly to her images, or how much her subsequent images respond directly to preverbs. They stand in undefined but strong

---

artist Ashley Garrett's miniature paintings in a work called *Co-Configurative Eternities: Preverbs for Ashley Garrett's Tarot Paintings* (Annandale-on-Hudson, NY: Metambesen, 2019), available online.

[15] Susan Quasha and Robert Kelly, *Winter Music* (Rhinebeck and Barrytown, NY: "T" Space Editions, in collaboration with Station Hill, 2014).

> and complex coperformative relation to each other, while retaining an essential independence. They seem to be in dialogue.

Chie Hasegawa's dreams or Susan Quasha's photographs—the collaborative process has a clear and evolving kinship. In both the photographs and the poems, the reader is invited into a situation where categories of being and relation are freshly renewed. Habitual frameworks insofar as they allow us to elude present awareness are continuously challenged without relapse into lyric formulations or strictures of narrative. Dreams, photographs, poems—perhaps these instances of collaboration give us a feel for how, in their nature, they all come to be:

> Think of here as where we go in where nothing gets through the same.
> There are spaces unconvinced of their orientation.
> This is where we come in as far as holding open.
>
> (*Hilaritas Sublime,* 30)

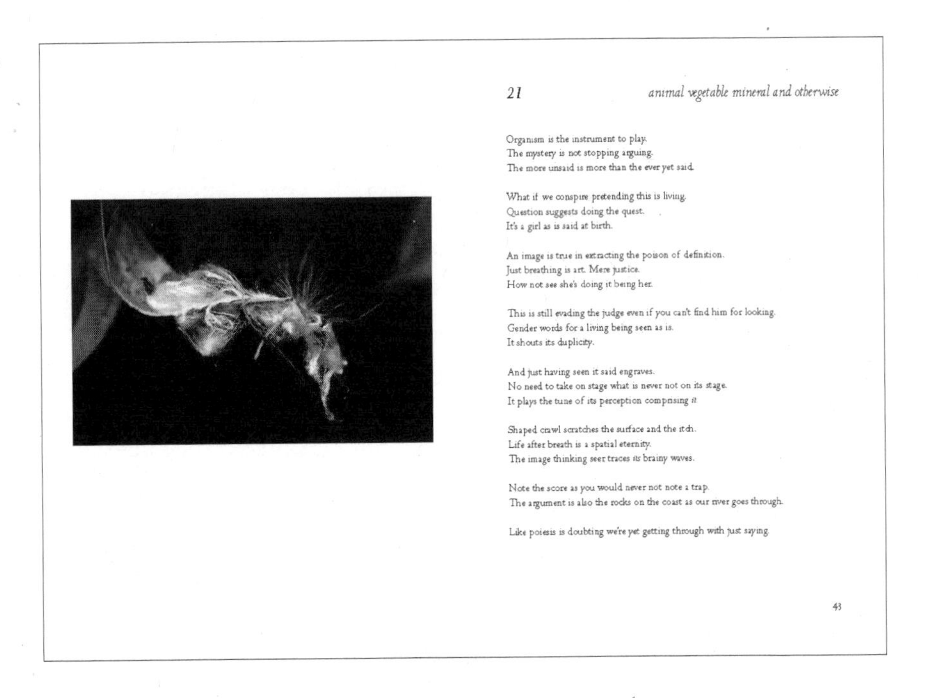

21 *animal vegetable mineral and otherwise*

Organism is the instrument to play.
The mystery is not stopping arguing.
The more unsaid is more than the ever yet said.

What if we conspire pretending this is living.
Question suggests doing the quest.
It's a girl as is said at birth.

An image is true in extracting the poison of definition.
Just breathing is art. Mere justice.
How not see she's doing it being her.

This is still evading the judge even if *you* can't find him for looking.
Gender words for a living being seen as is.
It shouts its duplicity.

And just having seen it said engraves.
No need to take on stage what is never not on its stage.
It plays the tune of its perception comprising *it*

Shaped crawl scratches the surface and the itch.
Life after breath is a spatial eternity.
The image thinking seer traces *its* brainy waves.

Note the score as *you* would never not note a trap.
The argument is also the rocks on the coast as our river goes through.

Like poiesis is doubting we're *yet* getting through with just saying.

43

Facing pages from Hilaritas Sublime *(2020), photography Susan Quasha/preverbs George Quasha*

Burt Kimmelman

George Quasha's Linear Music

There is such a thing as a George Quasha poetic line. What it is can be understood, essentially, by one particular aspect of it: its gravitational field. This field makes possible an inner integrity, the line's cohesive dynamic—a quality that has often been commented upon, including by Quasha himself. This cohesive, self-contained quality, furthermore, is a part of all his creations. In discussing his "axial stones" sculptures, he has spoken of "a poetics that favors *art acting at the boundary of its own definition*."[1] What is the nature of this coherence, exactly? The question returns our attention to his line. There has yet to be a full accounting of Quasha's line, however. What I hope to do here is to enlarge and deepen an appreciation of it.

To this end, let me begin by observing that, in particular, Quasha has wanted to claim, for his nevertheless unique practice of making poetry, the influence of William Blake's poetic practice; but there are also Blake's ideas about, and practice of, making visual art. For Quasha, key to Blake's philosophy of art and way of doing it is his notion of a "bounding line" (hence Quasha's use of the term "*boundary*," above). Meant specifically to demarcate the edge of a visual image on a canvas, the "bounding line," as a trope, possesses a potential still to be fully realized. And, seeing already how Quasha has appropriated it—in order to conceive of the *sui generis* work of art or poem—Blake's "bounding line" can provide insight into a body of modern poetry and theorizing I believe to have been equally important in Quasha's artistic, poetic development.

Blake's influence on Quasha has been enormous. Even so, Quasha's poetics, I am suggesting, is just as much a consequence of his knowing and reading near-contemporaries like Robert Duncan, Charles Olson,

[1] "The Axial," *Ecopoetics* 2.8 (25 November 2002), 112; hereinafter cited parenthetically. Cf. *Axial Stones: An Art of Precarious Balance*, foreword Carter Ratcliff, 2006.

John Cage, as well as other poets of the post-World War II avant-garde (whose roots go back to Modernist poets such as Ezra Pound). The gravitational force holding Quasha's lines and poems together comes as much or more from these people.

Quasha's poetic achievement emerges out of this welter of persons, ideas and aesthetics. What is remarkable is how his poetry has transcended it. To explain how this is so, I must turn back to Blake—specifically to that particular coinage of his, the "bounding line," which he used mainly to indicate that which is to be made distinct within a visual field (he meant it, specifically, to criticize the "blurring techniques" of earlier artists like Rembrandt and Rubens).[2] Even so, as Blake writes of this bounding line, it "distinguishes honesty from knavery." More largely, then, whatever its physical property, it is the "line of rectitude and certainty in" a person's "actions and intentions"—because "Every Line is the Line of Beauty."[3]

Blake's influence on Quasha is not merely to be located in his apprehension of form *per se*. It is true that Quasha's poems, his lines, do not depend on anything other than themselves—rather than in conjunction with his work as artist, musician, thinker, and serious t'ai chi practitioner. When contemplating the range of his creative activities, they seem to possess some common root, and in fact, for all normal intents and purposes they do; nevertheless, the poetry, the Quasha line, has to be considered solely on its own.

The possibly irresistible urge to include in one's assessment of Quasha's poetry something that might usually be considered extraneous to it, such as his work as visual artist, can arise from familiarity with his conceptualization of *axiality*—and here, too, Blake as an influence on Quasha should not be overlooked. While the "bounding line" for Blake was to be located principally in terms of visual art, Quasha as visual artist can think about poetry within the dimension of space as well as time. Additionally, he has developed his important concepts of *axis* and *axiality*, and these obtain to all of his imaginative activities. The axial,

---

[2] Samuel Foster Damon, *A Blake Dictionary: The Ideas and Symbols of William Blake*, rev. ed. (Hanover, NH: University Press of New England, 1988), 319.

[3] William Blake, *A Descriptive Catalogue* (Woodstock Books, 1809), xv.

for Quasha, is not merely physical (just as Blake took pains to qualify his "bounding line" as something more than technique or visual effect). Indeed, Quasha has derived his conceptualization of *axiality*, which informs his work both as poet and artist, in good measure from t'ai chi (yet, prior to his taking up this practice, he had been inspired by D'Arcy Thompson's thinking about "torsion" in his now famous morphological study, *On Growth and Form*).[4]

Axiality is key as it informs all of Quasha's artistic endeavors. It has played a generative role in his writing, Blake and Thompson salient within the Quasha ancestry. A *bounding line* vividly, as it were, shows itself to be of great use in comprehending his oeuvre within which physical principles are integral to poetic and, more broadly, aesthetic matters. The gravitational field in Quasha's verse line is not limited to the linguistic intrinsically—even as its presence is felt through the words of the line, through strings of words, through syntax. Moreover, the "sense" of his typical line-length statement is not limited to the music of the line, as might be true for poetry valued usually as such. It is that Quasha's singular, stand-alone line is not, in some prosaic sense, explicative. The palpable quality of a single Quasha line, more often than not—a single line on the page standing on its own, as distinct and intact—derives especially from its pithy quality, and, thereby, the line, possessing an extraordinary individuality, may not easily relate to surrounding lines.

A *bounding line*, accenting visual figuration, becomes a line that bounds across the page or, when read aloud, across the time of an

---

[4] Quasha used the two vol. edition, D'Arcy Wentworth Thompson, *On Growth and Form* (Cambridge: Cambridge University Press, 1959), II, 887-892, "A Further Note on Torsion," describing the growth of vines around an axis; Quasha applied this dynamic morphological analysis to Blake's Minor Prophecies in "Orc as a Fiery Paradigm of Poetic Torsion," in David Erdman and John T. Grant, *Blake's Visionary Forms Dramatic* (Princeton: Princeton University Press, 1970), 263-284; available online: www.academia.edu. The currently available single vol. edition is *On Growth and Form: The Complete Revised Edition* (Mineola, NY: Dover, 1992). Quasha's practice of "axial drawing" began in 1972 following a psychedelic experience, which spurred his eventual focus on proprioception (email to author, 4 August 2021).

utterance.[5] And, the fact is, all of Quasha's creative activities are present within his verse line, in a synergy. Another way of saying this might be that the line performs a dance. Like t'ai chi, dance exists simultaneously on both the spatial and temporal planes. Furthermore, dance occurs within a gravitational field. Quasha has said that his "'measure' is proprioceptive," and he has spoken of a "field proprioception." Here, then, is a primary source of Quasha's prosody. What he has called the "torsion principle," when applied to Blake, becomes the "axial principle" of the preverbs ("The Axial," 112). This notion will later extend to "ecoproprioception."

The utterance of the preverb line is frequently a single breath. Quasha's linearity—as it has come to its fullness within the multi-volume preverbs project—takes the form of the singular, self-contained gesture. Yes, of course, it has its music, which one might sense comes from dance or, more fundamentally, from the human body's movement—that is to say, *proprioception*. It is this music I find most remarkable, inasmuch as it resides within writing.

Quasha's poems, whose energy exudes from his syntax, have managed to elude the trap of language—unlike the work of his predecessor poets. In this way his lines, not simply music, do not merely possess the quality of the poetic. More to the point, his lines make the poetic the foreground of their reader's experience. To be sure, they foreground themselves as poetry. The Quasha poetic line is poetry; it also *performs* it.

The *preverbs* project began, Quasha has said, "as a way of reflecting on and within William Blake's 'Proverbs of Hell' [wherein the] wisdom proverb is inverted, breaking convention to recover 'wisdom' as a non-dogmatic state of visionary—let's say *gnoetic*—apperception."[6]

---

[5] As Walter Ong first showed, both systematically and dramatically (in *Orality and Literacy: The Technologizing of the Word* [1982, Oxfordshire, UK: Routledge, 2012]), human language, certainly preceding literacy (albeit Ong's insight refers to language making and comprehension in the present as well) involves the whole person whose physicality is integral to the process of communication and meaning making.

[6] "Pre Gnoetic," *The Daimon of the Moment (preverbs)*, 2015, 133; hereinafter cited parenthetically.

It is worth observing that the proverbs, providing a foundation for the creation of Quasha's preverbs (cf., e.g., "pre" in *Things Done for Themselves*),[7] do not much rely on the comma. The preverbs mostly abjure it. Reminiscent of Blake's lineation in the proverbs, the preverbs often take form, moreover, in luxuriantly long lines. There are counter phrases in shorter lines; and the shorter lines do contain commas that, relative to them, are rare in the long lines. In any case, a number of these long lines embody the basic impulse to be found within Quasha's poetic music.

Here is one of Blake's generously long lines, with which Quasha may have been especially enamored:

> If the fool would persist in his folly he would become wise.

Here's another:

> The most sublime act is to set another before you.

For all their sententious core—which is there to be heard in the preverbs—Blake's lines surprise their reader in what they propose. The fact that they are propositions does not go unnoticed.

Of course, Blake is working out of a historical long-line tradition. This tradition includes, for instance, Virgil's *Aeneid*, which can be seen and heard in these opening lines:

> Arma virumque cano, Troiae qui primus ab oris
> Italiam, fato profugus, Laviniaque venit
> litora, multum ille et terris iactatus et alto
> vi superum saevae memorem Iunonis ob iram.

Virgil's first three lines give way to the fourth, completing a syntactic unit. A momentum carries the ensemble to completion. Likewise, here are the opening lines of Whitman's *Song of Myself*; note the near absence of a caesura in the longer lines:

> I celebrate myself, and sing myself,
> And what I assume you shall assume,

---

[7] *Things Done for Themselves (preverbs)*, 2015, 175.

For every atom belonging to me as good belongs to you.
I loafe and invite my soul,
I lean and loafe at my ease observing a spear of summer grass.

In *Song of Myself* Whitman's very structure is devoted to the long line, whose symbolism and even feel both exemplify the optimism of the poem's speaker and connote the breadth of the American continent. The very long fifth line (above) contains no comma. It's not missing.

Some of the *Proverbs*' long lines unfold with their needed pauses; some purposively are not meant to tarry. Here's a Quasha preverb, in answer to the first of Blake's proverbs I've quoted (above):

You won't catch me lazing about in wisdom.
"Only the Truly Living Can Truly Die,"
The Daimon of the Moment, 52

Or take this longer line whose sentiment is, relative to Blake's line, more tenuous while it shares his outlook:

Looking for a line that has not yet occurred to not miss a future
world long visible. (52)

As for the second quoted line by Blake (above), here is a likely response, which is more intimate, just as authentic:

How can I address the you who is only now you? (53)

Here is a whole preverbs poem, "Playing Out"; it is beautifully symmetrical in its entirety, as it flows, ebbs, and flows:

Stand on principle at the precipice lest it get away.
A line, a flow, a sphere, a little fear, blink! Surrounded.

This black-and-white mystery is that we are enjoined to be here.
Surf her a letter at a time.
Life in the cursive green room rimes high, free-running beyond strife.

Line up a sail to propel us between nothing and something.

Glance flows, cloud shows, graph trail knows.

(*Verbal Paradise*)[8]

The longer lines (ll. 3 and 6, even l. 5), extended beyond a reader's expectation, establish both the speaker's presence and what Quasha might call his "pre-wisdom" voice ("Pre Gnoetic," 133).

In thinking about the hexameter tradition, simply in the juxtaposition of Quasha's luxuriously long lines—as they are counterpoised within a greater musical rhetoric—we acknowledge what the hexameter has done for poetry overall, especially once poetry comes to exist more in its written than oral milieu—taking into account the logical operations literacy establishes. The forerunner of the syllogism that is a product of literacy is the memorable verbal formulation. Along with rhyme and meter, preliterate poetry's prosody, as it were, consisted of epithets and other phrasings and formulas created to serve as a matrix within which the *sceop* or *griot* could place information for retrieval upon occasion. The syllogism proper, however, not so unlike the wisdom proverb hearkening back to preliterate times, emerges only with literacy's higher-order abstract thinking that makes it possible. The preverbs, which are exquisitely literate, undo the literacy-orality hierarchy. Nevertheless, we find in them the capacity for abstraction; and, remarkably, it is this capacity that allows for a purchase on dreaming.

Quasha has thought a lot about dreaming, and I would say it is a driving force for him. We might contemplate the phenomenon of dreaming after hearing or reading Quasha's preverbs—we who are, paradoxically, alienated from our very dreams by our literate consciousness. In "Oneiropoeia: Telling Tales on Dreaming," a prose commentary in *Ainu Dreams*, Quasha writes that "[n]othing is more tantalizing than the dream as an 'object' of thought, because it won't stay still. It won't even stay *there*. Its nature as *object* seems to end up challenging the nature of objects."[9] We can refer to this situation as a condition of alien-

---

[8] *Verbal Paradise (preverbs)*, 2011, 23.

[9] Quasha with Chie (buun) Hasegawa, "Oneiropoeia: Telling Tales on Dreaming," *Ainu Dreams*, 127, and online; hereinafter cited parenthetically.

ation, in the grandest sense the condition of civilization as we know it, which could not have come about without the spread of literacy (again, as Walter Ong, and a great many other scholars, have shown).

The preverbs return us, so to speak, to our unconscious. They are certainly visual, and yet their recovery of an essence of human being involved in and signaled by dreams has to do with time and gravity. "[Dream] seeks a free and easy dance partner," Quasha maintains, one "capable of reserving a power of all possible dances, yet a power understood by no one" (128). Time depends on gravity, and it is this dimension, in the preverbs, which we feel in the movement of Quasha's poetic line.

This movement, however, will mean ultimately subverting the impulse Blake harnessed and made his own. Quasha's "poem may need to suspend certain of its own merely familiar modes of self-awareness" (128). Blake's proverbs, in their irony, are meant to get beneath the easy logic of the apothegm. Quasha's preverbs, in their utter charm having to do with something other than irony, send us back to confronting the human dilemma of language. As Jacques Derrida writes at the start of *Of Grammatology*: "[h]owever the topic is considered, the problem of language has never been simply one problem among others."[10] Quasha will insist that "[d]ream is language, and all attempts to understand language as necessarily different from dream impoverish both language and dream. Dream's refusal to speak points toward a truth of language, the 'failure' of language to disclose" ("Oneiropoeia," 129).

A Quasha preverb (pre-verb, pre-logic, pre-pragmatic) reawakens, releases, from the confines of language, of written language, the force of dream and therefore human essence. Theories of art, literature, music, dance, which hold that we make art in order to come to terms with our mortal state, stupendously overlook the profoundly vivid reality of dream consciousness as well as the fact that art is the attempt to cope with dreaming, certainly to commune with our dreams. Quasha knows enough not to get into that wrestling match with the dream (*pace* Freud) in trying to make sense of it. Rather, Quasha has constructed an access to dreaming. To say this is not to dismiss the preverbs as being mere

[10] Jacques Derrida, *Of Grammatology*, tr. G. C. Spivak (Baltimore: Johns Hopkins University Press, 1976), 6.

tools for living, though. Quite the opposite, the preverbs are poetry in its purest form—for that matter they could be a purer form of verse—and thereby they are not suited to the practical efforts necessary in order to live in any commonplace sense.

In thinking about dream, dance, gravity, I would set alongside Blake's proverbs, which might be viewed as a source of revelation for Quasha, what I think has been an equally generative text for him: Robert Duncan's poem "Often I Am Permitted to Return to a Meadow." Duncan's "place of first permission" in the poem's penultimate line has, for me, always alluded to the domain of the dream, the unconscious. This poem does not merely represent the engagement by a young George Quasha with the poetry and poetics of the later North American avant-garde. In this respect, both Quasha's and Duncan's work ought to be considered in tandem with that of Charles Olson. Olson's "open field poetics" is enacted in Duncan's poem that is a mainstay in his volume *The Opening of the Field*. Olson's own "projective" poetry, as well as his game-changing essay "Projective Verse," sponsor both Quasha and Duncan. Then, too, there is Olson's essay "Proprioception." George and Susan Quasha were friendly with both Olson and Duncan. They could not have avoided any of these works; in fact, they have acknowledged strong interest in these particular works on occasion.

Olson's poetry, on the other hand, for all its prosodic grandeur, is not the inspiration for Quasha's preverbs nor the model Duncan's poetry provides. "Often I Am Permitted to Return to a Meadow," recalling the hexameter tradition, catches the reader up—in part due to its long, flowing lines, the longest of them being the poem's title preceding "as if it were a scene made-up by the mind"—in a realm of enchantment (the phrase "as if" doing its work), a realm in which a human being is at one with the world. Dream is not sequestered within this world, or otherwise minimized. Yet the poem's irresistible momentum is equally due to those long lines. The poem's unfolding underwrites the momentum *within* the line that we find in Quasha's preverbs (as well as some poems in his precursor volume, *Ainu Dreams*).

Duncan's choice to use the word "chaos," in the antepenultimate line ("certain bounds" that resist the "chaos"), creates an interesting proposition. Is it the lack of rules—or might we say the rules of dream do not comport with those of the conscious, rational mind whose very rationality is used in trying to approach the mystery of dreaming? The dream state will not allow the operations of the logical mind. Hence our waking life, that which the literary apothegm trades upon—even Blake's version of it—is a chaos in and of itself, in relation the flow of a life force that is part of the natural world, that world out of which the human psyche evolves.

"Often I am Permitted" might serve as an *ars poetica* for Duncan. In a peculiar, interesting way it is what comes to be Quasha's poetics. The conduit, the preverb ("pre wisdom"), involves the physical body as well as the metaphysical mind. The natural, visible, tactile world in Duncan's poem—the dance of "ring a round of roses"—strives to be one with the psyche, to posit a world as a place that makes room for dream, for the unconscious.

Quasha fulfills Duncan's attempt. His preverbs reside organically within such a world to which the poet enjoys some access. Of course, neither Quasha nor Duncan is working in hexameters; yet there is the sense of the luxurious, expansively long line. Perhaps Pound's first Canto, its opening seven lines, beginning with "And then went down to the ship," may very well have served as a baseline for Duncan's prosody. Duncan's lines express a sense of communion and revelation; Pound's lines embody a determination in the face of debacle in order to fulfill a prophecy (Pound wishing to reprise both Homer's and Virgil's epic poems). Each set of lines has its own, appropriate, meter and verbal music.

What there is less of in Pound's poem, in contrast to Duncan's, in any case, is the sense of the breath as measure, such as Olson spells out in "Projective Verse":

> [...] the syllable is only the first child of the incest of verse (always, that Egyptian thing, it produces twins!). The other child is the LINE. And together, these two, the syllable and the line, they make a poem, they make that thing, the—what shall we call it, the Boss of all, the "Single Intelligence." And the line comes (I swear it) from the breath, from the breathing of the man who

> writes, at the moment that he writes, and thus is, it is here that, the daily work, the WORK, gets in, for only he, the man who writes, can declare, at every moment, the line its metric and its ending— where its breathing, shall come to, termination.
>
> The trouble with most work, to my taking, since the breaking away from traditional lines and stanzas, and from such wholes as, say, Chaucer's Troilus or S's Lear, is: contemporary workers go lazy RIGHT HERE WHERE THE LINE IS BORN.
>
> Let me put it baldly. The two halves are:
>
> the HEAD, by way of the EAR, to the SYLLABLE
> the HEART, by way of the BREATH, to the LINE[11]

In Olson's poems, his breathing is also appropriate to his vision and task ("Verse now, 1950 [must] put into itself certain laws and possibilities of the breath, of the breathing of the man who writes" ["Projective Verse"]). Here, for example, is the opening line of "I, Maximus of Gloucester, to You," which sets a pace: "Off-shore, by islands hidden in the blood [...]." When I was young, I heard Olson read his poetry aloud; his breathing was palpable. It made me realize, as Quasha must have realized, how not only autobiographical but also *visceral* Olson's poetics could be. (The reading, quite dramatic, emanated from a huge bulk of a man.)

Reinstating the body in poetry or song has been central, I would argue, to Quasha, and it was so for Duncan, comporting with Pound's concept of *melopoeia.* Olson would eschew the unbroken long line such as emerges out of the much older hexameter tradition, as if his own breathing dictated that choice. In contrast, along with Blake, Duncan, especially in his unbroken long lines, serves equally as a muse for Quasha, especially where he wishes to invoke the subconscious reality of the dream in the preverbs. This is a reality that writing itself has purportedly conceded to be beyond either its reach or task. Quasha's rhetoric of the

[11] Charles Olson, "Projective Verse" [1950], now available online and elsewhere.

apothegm, à la his other muse, Blake, is put to the purpose of an utterance that is at once deeply human and poetic, while, in its insistence as poetry, it succeeds in standing apart from language's ostensible function.

The preverbs are poetry in some essence, which, like all utterance burdened by words, manages statements that are beautiful and haunting as they bring into the now the imagination in and for itself. What the preverbs also do is to foreground the music of the human voice. This is Quasha's music, although readers get a sense of it as theirs—embodied in syntaxes we recognize as familiar even if, finally, we do so for reasons having nothing to do with the rational mind. The fact that his long lines are coherent unto themselves is what gives the preverbs their music as they come forth. They are a music that emerges from deep within the body as well as the psyche—a music, to quote Pound's "How to Read," which makes possible "the dance of the intellect."[12]

A Further Thought

Pound famously talked about poetry's three fundamental aspects: *phanopoeia*, *melopoeia*, and *logopoeia*. While this essay has focused primarily on Quasha's poetics in terms of melopoeia, I hasten now to address the logopoeic dimension in preverbs, which should be viewed as equally important, as regards how they involve processes of thinking and the effects thereof. In accounting for the lure and power of the preverbs' language, I have directed attention to the way in which the preverbs are grounded in bodily awareness, and so the body's responsiveness to gravity. The result is a unique species of poetry, certainly of poetic music; yet—as Quasha indeed likes to emphasize, this unusual music doing its own kind of thinking—the preverbs serve as an induction into a unique way of *reading*.

His aim, he has said, has been "to invite the reader to be co-creative in discovering new reading modalities." Another way he says this is: "The poet is the poem's first reader and the reader the ongoing poet of the text."[13] Perhaps the theoretical crux here involves the writtenness of

---

[12] Ezra Pound's "How to Read" (1918) in *The Literary Essays of Ezra Pound* (New York: New Directions, 1935), 15-40.

[13] Email to author (August 4, 2021), including this and further citations below.

the preverbs—that is, they are read on the page at least as often as heard aloud. Inasmuch as they take the form of inscription, to be sure, they necessarily involve a reader's intellectual engagement. No doubt, like all highly accomplished poetry, the preverbs do more than disclose a previously unrealized capacity of language; also, they create the possibility of poiesis itself.

Along with Duncan's "Often I am Permitted...," Quasha, in his mid-twenties, turned his attention to Duncan's "Structure of Rime" series of poems; this work, too, had a lasting impact on him, most especially at the level of syntax. In an email to me, Quasha quoted these lines of Duncan's: "I ask the unyielding Sentence that shows Itself forth in the language as I make it, / Speak! For I name myself your master, who come to serve. / Writing is first a search in obedience... / I saw a snake-like beauty in the living changes of syntax." Quasha's subsequent remembrance is telling: "When I read these lines I felt that my discovery of torsional syntax/structure in Blake had found its contemporary incarnation." Quasha continues as follows:

> I have no doubt that this laid the seeds of preverbs to come. These are the lines that granted a kind of primal permission to my 26 year old mind to accept the authority of unfolding language. It's interesting to consider how single lines—single sentences—can alter how we think of and use language.

The power of language—to be sure, its crucial role in human affairs (à la Derrida's comment quoted above—which comes early in his pivotal work *Of Grammatology*, especially with respect to écriture)—resides in what Pound called *logopoeia*, and it should go without saying that this aspect of poetry, as it manifests in Quasha's preverbs, is absolutely crucial.

Yet it is also true that poetry, unlike, say, painting or the other visual arts, exists on the temporal plane along with music. Paradoxically, this distinction, when contemplating Quasha's achievements, is best exemplified in his axial stones sculptures. They would not be possible without the force of gravity. As Quasha writes, "the *rising* force that gravity inspires is its contrary, the vertical rebound, the *lift*, indeed the *levity*, in the art response."

beauty = optimal x precarious

Axial Stones #18 with preverb

William Benton

Two Handed Transcendence

Glossodelia Attract and *Axial Stones: An Art of Precarious Balance*

George Quasha's "preverbs" do what Frank O'Hara said about Abstract Expressionist paintings: they leave "the event of [their] passage."[1] In a continuum of lines, or line clusters, they move down the page like bright fractals. Here is a sample of a complete poem from *Glossodelia Attract,*[2] Quasha's ninth book of preverbs in a span of seventeen years.

giving sign to the space around

I wave my hand as I'm saying waving and the hand is drawing this
picture, it's real.
Setting the sun free in the brain lets a thinking shine in surround mind.
This is not a technique but a high-velocity turn with an urge to tell.

Thinking continuous surface is thinking itself.
I fell off an unknown side in a present tense situation and landed
here moving mind.
I reached the other side and realized it's this side.

Listen, there's a clinking in surround.

A thing is said on its own plane wherever it gets its information.
Desire recurrently urges us back, fearing loss, wanting what's
missed, loudly.

---

1 Frank O'Hara, "Franz Kline," *Art Chronicles, 1954-1966* (New York: G. Braziller, 1975), 40-52.

2 *Glossodelia Attract (preverbs)*, 2015; hereinafter cited in text parenthetically.

A wild dance of syntax barely shows on the other side of willing
reversals.
I feel myself going forward but the direction appears arbitrary.
Yet we always know when something is before us in surround world.

Anyone refusing to make sense until sense makes itself is in self-
avant-garde mode.
The sociology is that no one dares admit a free-standing truth.

In the dark of public light what cannot not be true hides from sight.
(*GA* 46)

If you write a line that is an enactment of its own becoming, you're probably a poet. If you write the same line in a hundred new, inventive ways, you're an evangelist. From the beginning pages of the book it's apparent that a singular program is underway. Some of the writing in these preverbs can have an intimate, stand-alone pulse, almost like a Creeley poem, yet instead of being broken into measures of breath, each pushes off in a single, horizontal trajectory. A different ordering and attitude is at work.

The structure of the book itself reflects this. The text of each poem fills a page, but, like an imposed stop, the end of the page ends the poem. Each poem is numbered and titled. The book is 150 pages long and divided into seven sections. But these divisions, or decisions, seem little more than an arbitrary parsing out of abundance. The lines are forthcoming, one senses, almost at will. This is perhaps the most astonishing aspect of Quasha's preverbs. Each poem, rather than evolving from a discrete source of its own, seems to riff forward from the starting point of a title. It's like a Niagara of hieratic energy.

These are poems that turn their own originality inside out. They write on the veil they lift and dance a step or two beyond our reach.

Quasha is first a poet, but also makes drawings, paintings, and sculpture, all of which are connected by what he calls "axial composition." In his paintings, which grew out of graphite drawings (which grew out of the poems), he loads two brushes, each with multiple pigments of closely related earth tones and, using both hands at the same time, paints a single, spontaneous intertwining swath that runs down the central axis of the page. One can imagine the gesture as something like the hands of a magus in midair.

Axial Drawing (graphite, two-handed), 2005

At first glance, the result seems too elegant, too effortless, and too slight. Also the marks themselves resemble tropes of flourish and arabesque, which give the image a decorative feel. Yet these shortcomings are in part offset by the concept of the work, which stresses the importance of the axial. The paint, moving in formal variations around a single axis, answers to a system other than establishment aesthetics. In this sense, the pictures are a kind of Outsider Art, not as a consequence of primitive skills, but by acting on precepts that have their roots in other disciplines.

In *Axial Stones*, an impressively put together book illustrated with color plates,[3] Quasha's sculpture approaches exactly a mainstream threshold. Basically, these are found stones, picked up by Quasha and his wife Susan along the banks of the Hudson, or in other nearby areas. Two, and sometimes three stones are stacked one on top of another until a precarious but perfect balance is found—a "still point," as Quasha says. This still point becomes the reveal of an invisible axis around which, like the "zip" in a Barnett Newman painting, the piece coheres. Metaphors of mating, destiny, and so forth come to mind. Quasha has exhibited the sculptures in galleries. No connective rods or adhesives are used. Gravity is the sole force that holds a work together. Its form is the condition of its grace; its grace the condition of its form.

Quasha came of age as a poet in the sixties and seventies, with the Pound-Williams-Eliot-Stevens inheritance, Black Mountain College, The New York School, Eastern Thought, and John Cage in the air. It was a time, in the decade following Charles Olson's landmark essay *Projective Verse*, of defining statements and cosmologies of poetry. Much of Quasha's text in *Axial Stones* concerns itself with the concept of the axial. It is deeply founded and illuminating, but also at times unremitting in its attenuation. He writes:

> And I understand this provisional state to be the open domain of a non-definitive saying that performs what it addresses—the performative indicative.

---

[3] *Axial Stones: An Art of Precarious Balance*, foreword Carter Ratcliff, 2006; hereinafter cited in text parenthetically.

We know more or less what this means, but it has the feel of staying too long at the fair. You want to ask yourself: is ground lost, or gained, by converting process into the synthesis of a transcendent principle? Louis Zukofsky, in the beginning of "A-12," offers one answer:

From my body to other bodies
Angels and bastards interchangeably
Who had better sing and tell stories
Before all will be abstracted.

Yet Zukofsky's counsel comes—albeit as lines of poetry—in a passage that elucidates his own poetics.

Quasha's text gets more interesting when he talks about his actual work with stones. It takes on the aura of an adventure story, a mixture of Tolkien, totemism, and Tom Sawyer that would lose much of its sweep in paraphrase or excerpts. In the same way that the transcendent requires our witness as its primary element, Quasha treats his experience as the essential event, to which the stones serve as gnomic testimony.

How something is made can—and perhaps should—always be sui generis. But the thing made has to take its chances in the great world beside other things. Quasha's text is an extensive delineation of his process. "Beauty = optimal x precarious" is a repeated mantra. Mystical thought, supported by Quasha's knowledge of Buddhism and his association with Eastern teachers, plays an important role in his focus. Stones are at times sentient, with their own volition. What they "want" and "don't want" is respectfully considered. This is, of course, simply a quaint way of speaking, but on another level it is the armature for metaphors that deepen the experience of both process and self-seeking.

What we know about Quasha's sculptures changes everything about them except their appearance. If they were stuck together with superglue in the exact same arrangements, we wouldn't find them as compelling as we do. As a matter of fact, they would have the "artful" look of an exercise. They hold our attention by being performers in a *Cirque de Conceptuel*. We marvel at their precarious balance and assign to it, by conflating one with the other, the authority of an aesthetic value.

Quasha's immersion in process and the persuasion of his lucid, agile prose acts almost like a magician's misdirection, keeping the viewer's focus on the trick. At the same time he anticipates points of potential dissent and finesses or deflects them away. One good example, toward the end of the book, is uttered almost as an exit line, with the door swinging shut: "The work as event realizes a certain state, as if suddenly showing through" (*Axial Stones*, 153). This is a nod from the trenches of process at completion—that "certain state," in which process becomes irrelevant, art becomes art, and stands alone, beyond all contingency.

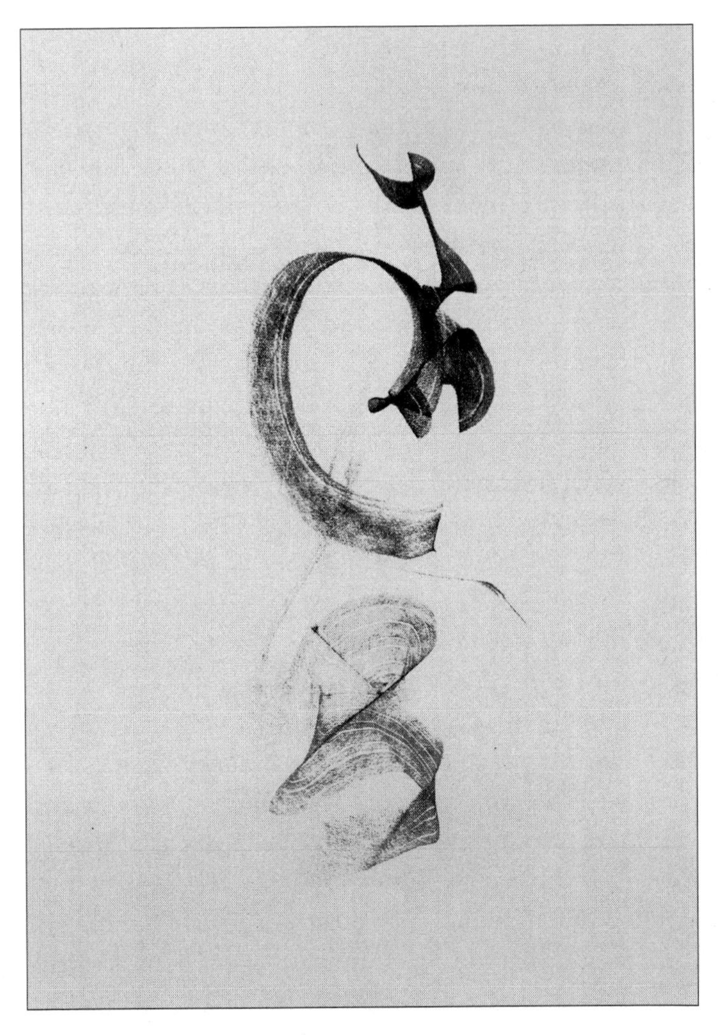

Axial Drawing (graphite, two-handed), 2005

Andrew Joron

On Quasha's Axial Stones

Thinking of George Quasha›s *Axial Stones* project, I am reminded of the long tradition of poets handling stones, in both the figurative and literal sense of "handling." Stones want to be touched both by the poet's words and by the poet's hands. *Touch me*—two words that summarize the aim and origin of art. Stones especially tell words that they have weight. Some stones cannot be moved by human hands alone. Are there words like this?

Some stones seem to float in midair. The Earth is one such stone, hanging over an infinite abyss. Every stone stands for the entire Earth, just as words stand for things. The weight of a stone results from the attraction of all other stones (the weight of a word, from all other words).

Quasha's axial stones stand in precarious balance. They present an exquisitely fine moment in time: they are about to fall, but they have not yet fallen. To be alive is to inhabit that moment. The axial stones conduct gravity: they guide it to the point where its hold on stone is made visible. We can watch the fingers of gravity playing—wondering, momentarily baffled—at the precise point where the two stones meet. In time, gravity will pull the stone down. But it has not yet figured out how to do so.

Quasha has written a fraction in stone, challenging gravity to solve it. The top stone is the numerator, the lower the denominator. If the denominator were zero—as it sometimes is—the solution would be infinity, where the numerator-stone, the Earth-stone, falls forever into the void. Kant, who had no idea of the expanding universe, considered a static cosmos in which the stars must be poised perfectly, the attraction of each canceling out that of the others—if this were not the case, the stars would gravitate toward one another, collapsing in a universal conflagration. Quasha's stones stay, even as they say, even as they perform the way a thought holds at bay, this cosmic collapse.

Gravity-defying stones are represented also in much of Paul Celan's late poetry. As Jason Groves points out in his essay "'The Stone in the

stones on edge draw attention equal to the space around

Axial Stones #33 with preverb

Air': Paul Celan's Other Terrain," Celan's frequent referencing of stones works, paradoxically, against the solidity and stability that stones imply—works against, indeed, the premise of referential language itself. Celan's poems

> not only do not mimetically strive to achieve for their language the material properties of stone (earthiness, density, durability, thingyness, etc.), properties in which a poetic language, cognizant of its own porosity and insularity, could seek refuge from the play of the textual; moreover, the poems disallow themselves to even imagine stone as possessing those properties in the first place. They dwell, rather, on the air in stones and stones in the air.[1]

As Celan writes in *The No-one's Rose* (1963),

> The bright
> stones travel through the air, white ones,
> the light-bringers.
> They want
> not to descend, not to crash,
> not to make contact.[2]

The "absent ground" in Celan's poetry receives figuration as a stone in the air. Likewise, Gustaf Sobin's 1984 poetry collection *The Earth as Air* consciously extends Celan's trope of aerial stones. Sobin's poetry of erasure and dispersal imagines substance—the earth itself—as precipitating out of sound-vibration: "that the earth be but the dark, sparkling residue of that blown emanation."[3] Once again, earth or stone is held poetically to participate in the qualities of air.

Of the four elements, earth has always been—compared to air, water, fire—considered the least susceptible to change and motion. This

---

[1] Jason Groves, "'The Stone in the Air: Paul Celan's Other Terrain,'" *Environment and Planning D: Society and Space* 29, June 2011, 470.

[2] In Groves, 477; trans. attrib. Paul Celan, *Selected Poems and Prose*, trans. John Felstiner (New York: Norton, 2001), p. 176.

[3] *The Earth As Air* (New York: New Directions, 1984), 97.

prejudice can be corrected by zooming out to longer timescales at which mountains flow like waves. (Whitehead's line, "A rock is a raging mass of activity," appears as the epigraph of one of Quasha's recent poems.)[4] Heraclitus did not exempt earth from his dictum that "everything flows." Such timescales are locked inside every stone. Quasha's axial stones not only allude—as signs—to these different levels of time, they *act upon* time, stretching the instant to accord with the "long now" of the stones' interiors.

Quasha's axial stones stand there as impossible objects, their balancing act almost a violation of nature. They are caught in an instant of precarity that strains time to the breaking point. Like us, they are always already about to fall.

A word about the implications of standing stones for poetic form: it was known to prehistoric peoples that setting up stones in defiance of gravity was a way of amassing power. Such earth-magic is also felt in the *bourrie* constructions of southern France: dome-like stone huts built as agricultural storehouses in the Middle Ages (one is depicted on the cover of Sobin's *Earth as Air*). These huts have held their shape for centuries, yet their stones are held together not by mortar but by the weight that each stone exerts upon every other. Similarly, in a poem, the weight of each word presses upon the presence of every other word, making—out of the gravity of meaning—a perpetual-motion machine.

Hence Quasha will write "Sequence is a pressure from outside time" in his book *Verbal Paradise*. Or in the same book: "*If you knew what the poem is you'd stone it.*" The direct address here is likely not only to a society that would judge and punish poetic transgression, but as well to the poet's own making, attesting to the act of *poiesis* as something as primordial as the infall of cosmic stones that created earth.

---

[4] Epigraph to "Verbal Paradise Is Not a Turn Away," *Verbal Paradise (preverbs)*, 2011, 16.

Charles Stein

George Quasha's *Preverbs*

One might recall that Augustine's deepest probings into the matter of "eternity" occur in his attempt to understand how our relation to both time and what is not time are involved in the act of reading a text. George Quasha's *preverbs* enact within the reader's attention an atemporal exigency through language. Playing intra-syntactically upon the intimacy between time and linguistic structure, Quasha's lines and fields of lines fold and wrinkle wavelets of a level of being that he often refers to as "undertime." What is unveiled is returned at once to its appropriate obscurity in moment after moment of utterance whose mode of declaration provokes the concrete coursing of our thinking toward a certain gaiety of inescapable inquiry.

What is it that is suspended across the vanishing interval between a phrase, whose meaning shimmers, hesitates, and sometimes insists even as it deliquesces within that interval, and a new phrase, which resonates the first with an ever-efflorescing transformation of sense? It is as if the lion's roar of awakening rumbled forth in the mute but eloquent interstices between ordinary morphemes—where the syllables that carry meanings are also vocables, but vocables that percolate intimations of the meaning of meaning itself.

I think what distinguishes Quasha's *preverbs* from other poetry is that the lines of these poems depend in a remarkable way on the concrete acts of reading them, in the very moment that these occur, whether we are gazing at the page silently or uttering them out loud to ourselves or one another.

Something like a twofold program or implicit agenda emerges: that the work must induce its discoveries upon or pass all the way over to the reader; that it must refuse the antitheses between content and occasion, between intelligence as disembodied thought and concrete sentience as fully embodied but deratiocinated presence.

So much here seems ambiguous, multi-valent, polysemous. One hears a thing meant, but then it shifts and means something else. It is tempting to try to gather these meanings, to decide between them or hear them together, to produce for oneself a thought surmounting them or including them all. But I think this is often to miss their most radical possibility: there is an edge between no meaning and too much meaning, and events on this edge might be inhabited just as they occur to us, in us, *as* us.

Thus I would suggest that we not try too hard to prepare ourselves to read these pieces, but rather we should read them with the idea of introducing ourselves to the concretely open instance of our reading them, moment to moment, and to each other, giving ourselves permission to hear them, to dwell in the questioning of them, even letting ourselves repeat them, pausing within and around them.

Don't do anything TO them, to PERFORM them.

Responsibility

The following is a way to see Quasha's *preverbs'* precarious situatedness among their own cognitive and ontological emanations:

Our poets' capacities to invest in their own invention (I mean how they wear the garments of their poetry, not how they expect to profit from it) relates to what attitude we take towards our own ontological originarity. (Ontological originarity: the not so obvious circumstance that *how being seems* depends on each of us. *How being seems* is the site of a precarious poetic responsibility: responsibility for the reader—who will become implicated in the work's sense of what seems to be—and responsibility to the further life of the poetic content.) If poets treat their own invention ironically—i.e., by disavowing its ontological force—well then, what the reader gets to "put on" is that PUT-ON, that irony. When poets intend the literal assertion of their imaginings, the work becomes a work of enthrallment —enchanting if you find it so—but a kind of binding-spell to freeze the reader's ontological will and align it to the specific orders of the poem's take on what is.

To release the poem from these two boondoggles—ironical disavowal and ontological fundamentalism—is where the intellectual responsibility of the poetry lies and where the ontological seriousness of poetic practice must lodge itself.

Quasha's *preverbs* project is the continuous registration of one poet's shouldering of this responsibility.

The Trajectory of Literal Meanings

Literal meanings have envelopes of possible extraneous meanings or wisps of other thoughts that hang in there along with them.

The *preverbs* poet's art of articulation manages the micro-spaces among these main thoughts and their extras.

Even the lines that seem to have but a single literal meaning often have auras accruing to them by the evanescent fields of thoughts in which they are tremulously situated.

The other thoughts that show these evanescent qualities resonate, accumulate, or produce atmospheres where *further other* thoughts flare and vamoose.

Self-reflection transitions to the intransitive. No unique sequencing can unscramble their cognitive inevitabilities.

Lines that seemingly "go flat" rather than satisfy a conventional expectation for prosodic harmony or rhythmic closure nevertheless enlist *pro*verbial diction for *pre*verbial intervention and allow further meanings to arise *via subtraction.*

The sense it doesn't make increases the *meaning scene.*

Consider the line "Language makes no promise to communicate." (*Glossodelia Attract*, 5) But what if in spite of it all, a missive from otherwhere were apparently delivered to my bewildered yet receptive understanding? Do we have here the fulfillment of a promise never made? But *can* language make promises and thereby show itself to be an active subject by denying it ever sent the letter received?

Multiple meanings may yield a complex of mutually implicating propositions; or: Instead of a multiplicity of positive meanings creating a polyphony of semiotic possibilities, a line might proliferate its own obscurities and then offer to clear them up by referring to them, or by inducing attention to the readerly events the line perhaps has just caused to occur.

Or the darkness itself might be made of a kind of light, the light of attention alert in cognition's darkness.

Ambiguities become local tools of the line and change as they are temporarily resolved in a given moment's reading.

Quasha's *preverbs* series not infrequently speaks of "seeing through." Here's a line from *Glossodelia Attract*: "This is the time of alternative obscurities to see through."[1]

To see through : as through a mist or some space of obscure cognition. To see through : as to overcome a deception.

But in either case, "see through" to *what*? And what "time" anyway is this "this"? Anything from the present historical moment to the present readerly event? Or the timeless time of the line itself? Or the *proverb*-time of the expression "Now is the time for all good men to come to the aid of their country"? The poet's line presumes to see through, say, such rhetoric, offering alternative obscurities to the obscure assertion of the proverb it denigrates and abuses.

Here an entire rhetorical, proverb-like construction suffers its variants.

Or this proliferation of possibilities might function more concretely than rhetorical ambiguities or even instances of polysemous polyphony or counterpoint. The mind must toggle among the sentence parts or among its own construals so that a kind of *movement* native to that line is allowed to occur. And the ambiguities or meaning possibilities occur as vibrations propagated by that movement--more ghosts and auras; meanings *in potentia,* affordances for readerly adventures.

---

[1] *Glossodelia Attract (preverbs)*, 2015, 5; hereinafter cited in text parenthetically.

The line about obscurities to see through is followed by:

Through thoroughly, as a word weighs.

One might return to the "seeing through" of the previous line, but, reading on, one just keeps on going. Thoroughly through with seeing through, further contemplations follow.

For instance, a sense of a certain lexigraphic resonance: "through" and "thorough" look like misprints of each other. Or: this lexigraphic self-penetration is itself a kind of salutary misdirection so that the ponderable matter of the lexigraphic items impends and measures: "weighs"—has weight—"weighs in" (like a boxer, possibly), measures what other matters pertain about it. But the line now wants to leave its previous ravishments behind and keep on going without sustaining the weight or momentum of the freight of cognitive baggage hefted up till now.

Every ontology enshrines principles of value. Conversely, where values are asserted, a correlative ontology is implied. Therefore, in work where ontology is emergent or tremulous or in process of being discerned, the very values that such work enacts—participates in, encourages, embodies—remain tremulous, in process, as well.

In the very matter of syntactical hesitation and invention, values appear and shimmer, disappear and are transgressed. And the reader is drawn into this play of ontology, meaning, and value, at the site where being, meaning and value are in play in his or her own being.

Axial Reading

> [...] *Axial*, a word I use somewhat idiosyncratically to call attention to a certain state of being—*free* being, or being coming into its natural state as free [...]. What is clear is that the axial is not a thing: not a philosophy; not a religion; not an aesthetic; in short, not itself any of the many ways that can be used to understand it. It's more like a space, a *worked* space—an intentional state of

> awareness in which something unpredicted occurs: a unique *event* resulting in what seemingly embodies its *origin* and yet itself is *original.* At once unchanging and nonrepeating.
>
> *Axial Stones: An Art of Precarious Balance*[2]

My remarks about an emergent or tremulous ontology (above) lead me to the following discussion of Quasha's axiality, which is for him a principle.

I want to say that axial writing induces axial reading.

If you think yourself competent to read, well, anything at all, your confidence in your competence might impede your reading of *preverbs.* An exaggeration no doubt, but consider: Slowing down the *pace* of reading, as one might do ordinarily in order to pick up nuance in a difficult passage, alters the sense of the text as you read it. Your cognitive faculty stutters, forgets what it thought to have thought but an instant before. Alternatively, reading *preverbs* at a normal pace may well make things slip by that you are aware that you are not aware of. It is almost as if a certain despair of understanding must set in, or a surrender, rather, to whatever it is that is happening in your reading mind, which cannot be grasped in advance of your struggle to understand it. The words go by, or you go by the words, and if the stars are right, a sense of meaning flashes.

Preverbial lines tend to break up inside the syntax they ride on, and in a way that not only plays upon the intimacy between time and syntax, but also inundates the mind with deep and turbid cognitive waters—waters that, as one continues to inhabit preverbial texts, begin to feel like they must have always secretly been churning both within syntax and within time. How *does* the beginning of a sentence—any sentence—conjoin to its end? How can what has already gone by—the first phrase of an utterance—be *altered* by what comes later? For it is not only the strangely disrupted morsels of preverbial language that exhibit this temporal anomaly, but ordinary language as well.

The categories of grammar that ordinarily identify the utterance one is confronted with are suddenly of little use. One reads, for instance,

---

[2] George Quasha, Prologue to *Axial Stones: An Art of Precarious Balance*, 2006, 20.

declarative sentences that function essentially in the mode of inquiry. The sentence is not asking a question syntactically, but the actual course of utterance induces an interrogative "mood"—a state of querulous openness in the very ground of one's intelligence. In this way, the phrase ceases to be an "object" that, through the spontaneous application of grammatical categories, one can identify and begin to understand; rather, its strange disequilibrium becomes a part of one's own cognitive apparatus. One becomes the "subject" of the utterance —not the grammatical subject and not the subject matter of the text but, instead, through a kind of axial induction, the text insinuates itself into one's own being at the sight where one utters speech and where one assumes the posture of understanding through the use of language. And again, this appears not as something peculiar to the language of *preverbs*, but something that might always have been true of ordinary declarative utterance, but in an unnoticed way.

Where syntax and time fold over on themselves and the very being of utterance shifts from object to subject, the deep relation between sound and sense, or in linguistic terms phonology and phonematics, seems to plummet into the poem's already turbid waters. "Vocables" are language-like sounds included in poems that do not function as morphemes—minimal units of meaning. Of course, poetry has always toyed with the borderland of linguistic sound—assonance, alliteration, rhyme, and rhythm; irrationalities, liminalities, twilights—teasing the noonday mind beyond the rational. But the interplay of "sound and sense" has generally worked to enfold the sounds of the poem up into the sense of the poem, so that these prosodic elements qualify or in other ways serve meaning, even if to render it ambiguous or polysemous. In this way, poetry reiterates the transformation of phonetic sounds into phonemic systems, a transformation that is supposed to be, according to the dominant school of linguistic theory, the very essence of language.

But in the disruptions of linguistic functioning in *preverbs*, an abyss opens in language such that the recuperation of sound by sense is *almost* suffered *not* to occur. The sounds of words do not actually function as vocables, as for instance in the sound poetry that Quasha has (as have

I) over the years sported with in abundance; but *almost* does so. With *preverbs* one must have an ear for an abyss without actually falling into it—or rather, without *only* falling into it. Or the falling occasions its own recovery (if it does), according to the reader's capacity to profit from the poem's ludic hazard. And, as in Nietzsche's famous remark to the effect that if you stare long enough into an abyss the abyss will stare back at you, it is almost as if in listening to that which opens in language through the preverbial exigency, language, at the edge of sound, and where objectivity itself has turned subjective, listens back. And why not? The activity of cognition no longer yields a thing cognized, but one's own experience inverts and, becoming itself thing-like… .

Authenticity and Simulation

I want to situate, if only for a somewhat extended discursive moment, one dimension of the *preverbs* within the ambience of a philosophical conundrum that has had enormous play in thinking about language and being over the last forty or fifty years—the problem of whether authenticity can be represented or even if it exists; whether appearances are merely simulacra. I think that the explorations enacted in *preverbs* may prove pertinent to this matter.

A noun may stand for a concept and a concept index the objects that fall under it; but if I want to think of the difference between a mental event as it actually occurs and the content of that event, a noun has a devil of a time assisting me in maintaining that difference, for although thought as I think it is a singular occurrence, it can re-occur: I can remember the moment of thinking it and I can repeatedly direct my attention to its concept—its informational content—without particularly focusing on its original occurrence.

If I distance my thought from the actual event in which it occurs, rendering it repeatable and capable of communication, even the most authentic thought, thus severed and served up for perusal or expression in language, becomes its own simulacrum. But a thought then *is* its simulacrum, not merely its occurrence. The *incapacity* of a noun to distinguish between a thought and its occasion is of its essence.

A corollary: A text both re-presents the occurrence that produced it and presents the informational content that authentically motivated its production. The poem (*pace* Wallace Stevens) is not only "the cry of its occasion, the very *res* itself," but *also* "about it."

Today the tendency to reduce all manner of things to their content as information is the last result of this coupling and uncoupling of thoughts from their occurrences. Information cannot distinguish authenticity, and this incapacity is of its essence. (Hence the famous Turing test that continues to addle the intelligence of *Matrix* aficionados.) We could say that the problematic concerning authenticity is the coupling of an immediate occasion with its information in such a way that the occasion remains distinguishable from its simulacrum, but that then the occasion vanishes into the trace that supplies its information, so the coupling cannot appear except as a distinction *within* information. There is information all the way down, until it disappears in a bottomless bottom, a passage beneath information where, *vis à vis* information, authenticity becomes logically ineffable. The authentic as the actual occasion of thought vanishes as well—into a subsequent occasion. However, the streaming of radically transitory occasions remains not only as a ghost to haunt information, but, were it to cease its haunting, as that which would spell the death of information itself. Information itself is a ghost, not only the authentic occasion of its content. But the ghost has its occasion too; thus the coupling.

The reign of the simulacrum involves the denial of the difference between the authentic and the simulacrum in this way: the authentic act and occasion of thought, if taken as an object and distinguished from its simulacrum, has already been removed from its authentic ground. If the evanescent occasion is indicated, referred to, treated as an object—even to declare its inauthenticity—then that treatment is already inauthentic. But then the accusation (*pace* Adorno) that authenticity is mere "jargon" stands on the same ground as the simulacrum itself. The indication that something is authentic (or inauthentic) is already verbalized, but the fact of its authenticity—that something (a thought, say) really did occur—is *liminal* to that verbalization. It does not fall on its own to the side of the simulacrum, but it cannot stand on its own through the assertion of some verbal token of it.

And yet it would speak.

Preverbs speak from and in and through the problematics of language and thought taken as occurrence and language and thought taken as content, inhabiting a liminal region that refuses reduction to either or neither or both.

To speak from that liminality—to hold to the authentic while recognizing its logical impossibility—cannot guarantee one's own thought's authenticity. *But such speaking can draw its interlocutors into the liminal realm,* where, as readers or hearers, they may discover within their own problematical being, the problematical arousal of intelligence actuated in its languaging.

All-Night Diner Quandaries

Glossodelia Attract 7: "Every thought rethinks reversing further" (11).
Glossodelia Attract 8: "Nothing is the way it's always been said" (12).

1

I cannot say what it means, even its many meanings, even its shifting senses. I can only report the meanings that in actual hearing arise in my mind, or seem to be called forth by me as I respond to their momentary impressions. I regard their trace in hearing them, reading them. I myself am personally drawn into the fractiousness and quandary of their poetry.

2

In trying to say what the poetry says I myself am drawn into the inquiry of saying what the poetry primarily is. I myself become the subject that inhabits the poetry.

3

First I hear it one way, then I check the trace of what I heard and hear it another. Then I make a move: I think I must choose how to negotiate the traces of these hearings. And *how* I choose conditions what comes next in the reading. Or no, I do not choose. I do not think that I must choose. Thus in my own way, the lines' time passes.

4

What I retain of one line—of the meanings I have allowed to come to cognition as I read it—conditions the very meaning context of what follows. And these conditionings either accumulate or dissolve, according to how I feel them accumulate or accumulate them, or feel them dissolve or dissolve them. In every attempt to describe this, the active and the passive change places.

5

Who is speaking in these lines? The trace of an inquiry into the relations between self and speech inhabits them essentially. But the readers play the line upon their private readerly instruments, becoming for the moment of reading, the speakers of them. The inquiry thus passes over from writer to readers, left to their own devices to conduct a further inquiry, along the lines the lines have opened.

6

Or, no, there is no inquiry. I stop, startled, and am happy with the interruption followed by a kind of light or lightness that *my* thought, inspired by the line, has effected. Next line, not so happy. The poet himself perhaps was not so happy, but left the line to sit there anyway, perhaps to further something unbeknownst to me, unbeknownst even to him, unbeknownst to my current reading.

7

Accumulation and recontextualization press their own delete buttons. One cannot in general say how the fielding of many lines in sequence functions. The light changes. The wind stops. But then one is in the Diner and the choice to recall the weather of a moment ago seems impertinent or doesn't seem at all. It was cold outside. Now you are warm. You are waiting for a menu. Now you choose among listed soups. Now you're eating pumpkins. The sequence is pertinent or not according to events / decisions you are the site of. Now it is Wednesday, back a week, remember? The weather and the pea soup mix and merge, enter into forgetfulness. The eruption of meaning in the mind compels its own time only, one time only.

8

I cannot give an accurate picture of what happens when I read a *preverb* without providing a complete report of my own being as I read it, and that is patently impossible. I can make a picture of what is happening as I read these lines, but that is another thing. I make a picture. But then I seem to enter into the poetics of the text by abject submission to its orderings, its ontological demands. And what I say is a trace, a record of such abjection.

9

Two impossibilities thus face off: that to give an account of the poems as if they were objects capable of adequate description is impertinent, impossible; that to present a concrete report of the spontaneous and reflective cognitive events that attend and in fact *are* that reading is also impertinent, impossible.

In this way *preverbs* inflect the impertinent, the impossible.

A New Imagination of Intelligence: An Addendum

Though the apparent stance of the language in Quasha's *preverbs* would seem to be what one might call an aggressive neutrality in regard to the many potentially volatile topics that are alluded to, *preverbs* nevertheless perform, as we have seen, a certain intervention upon the concrete mentality of its readers. This intervention is not without its possible effect upon the concrete condition of human intelligence quite generally, and therefore it is perhaps not remiss to add a few remarks regarding what I see as its historical relevance. The following is a first attempt to elaborate these matters, and I am well aware there is plenty more to think about regarding them.

We are living at a time in which the circumstance of public language itself has darkened and threatens to lose, if it has not already lost, what the medieval thinkers knew as "the good of the intellect." I need only mention the monstrous babel of electoral politics that we continue to suffer within, but also a confusion of tongues in philosophic discourse, in the becoming dubious of popular scientific writing through political and economic contamination, *and indeed* through the passing of a certain threshold of complexity in science itself that turns even critical and responsible thinking into factors contributing to their collective incoherence. Something like the emergence of *a new imagination of intelligence itself* is achingly called for.

The work toward this has been prepared by contemplative sciences and poetries and the inner work of art and other practices from immemorial times, though no single source for this necessary emergence can be articulated. What characterizes this preparation is an attention to the concrete processes in sensation and intellect, intuition and feeling (to evoke the four Jungian categories, just for the convenience and rough completeness of them) not so much as oppositions but as complements to the contents of these faculties. Whereas the Western intellect originating in fifth century Greece develops the abstract powers of thinking, disconnected from the concrete act of taking thought, to a degree that today seems almost to break off from the organic life that sponsors it (AI, robotics, etc.), ancient India treated intelligence primarily as a process of the concretely functioning mind. Mind in one cultural history came to mean the thing that produces adequate and logical texts, in the other what intensifies its own nature through concentration upon its immediate being. I want to say that the work of our time must be the bringing together of these modes of mentality: thought as perfection of representational content; thought as perfection of the inner ground of thinking. If that might occur in the production of texts, it would have to be through textual liminalities such as those evinced in the *preverbs*. The wish that such poetry might truly counterbalance the world-threatening aspect of science and its technologies (nuclear toxicity, global warming, the contamination of the ecosystem in innumerable ways, being the most obvious)—the wish that poetry might correct all this—may seem a forlorn dream, but work that transgresses the boundary between thought as act and thought as content and accomplishes this by suffusion, resonance, radiation, radiance, microdosing, and the setting of almost inaudible spells may indeed be the locus where such hope resides.

The practical site of this work would have to be interchanges between consciousness, intelligence, imagination, and speech that actually occur for each of us in our reading and hearing. I see Quasha's *preverbs* project as offering such a site, where, in not necessarily a merely small way, this work might be undertaken.

Cover of Not Even Rabbits Go Down This Hole (preverbs), *2020*

Matt Hill

George Quasha's Orphic Patina

Edges tend to be frontiers. Like some scout sussing out the unknown terrain ahead, George Quasha's project of *preverbial* poiesis indicates a fertile frontier found along the edges of life, of death, and of every event in between. He insists that we "inhabit the cracks." The cracks of course are the liminal thresholds that must be crossed in our own poetic journeys; irony and paradox rule the day in these headwaters of the preverbial flow.

Most acutely, in the fifth collection of preverbs published, *Not Even Rabbits Go Down This Hole*,[1] Quasha explores a multifaceted liminal world, where language creates a distinctly self-aware poetic reality as he saunters through known and unknown regions of self and verbal utterance. We watch this process of poem-making evolve as it happens along the preverbial edges, marked with the creases and folds that result in what Quasha terms "axial force." As he leads us through this adventure in "self-knowing," the bold lines manifest through the very nature of this poetic self-questioning. An Orphic patina surfaces across many of these poems, where balance and entanglement dance in poetic flux; where ontological/poetic values of truth-in-language are indicated by balance and discovery.

The preverb, as "precarious language act, an event at the edge that remains on edge in the reading" ("Pre," *Things Done For Themselves*),[2] is "a one liner that projects a particular state of language in the act of finding itself here and now." The preverb is also *previous* to wisdom, yet willingly still attempts "to state enduring truth." One stays in the "pre" state with

[1] *Not Even Rabbits Go Down This Hole (preverbs)*, 2020; hereinafter cited in text parenthetically.

[2] *Things Done for Themselves (preverbs)*, 2015, 176; *Glossodelia Attract (preverbs)*, 2015, xi; hereinafter cited in text parenthetically.

"right reading"—and "right" here means anything but correct; "Pre is the state in which preverb lives" ("Pre Gloss," *Glossodelia Attract*). There is no single correct interpretation of a preverb; its reading is somewhere between intuitive and instinctual, a traveling done along the edges of axial action. Since reading is an act of doing, it is also a proprioceptive act that moves across as awareness.

Whereas a proverb is a preformulated idea that proffers advice, a preverb makes no such offering. "Preverbs are readymades found in the shiftily lingual mind" (*Not Even Rabbits,* 123). A proverb can be a general observation on life, and many preverbs seem to share in this rhetorical attitude. Proverbs generally have long word-of-mouth histories, with origins obscured by the passing of generations. Yet "... preverbs can reorient the mind by shifting conceptions of what language is. Unlike proverbs, preverbs never claim to embody wisdom as such nor to transcend uncertainty" ("Pre Gloss," *Glossodelia Attract,* xi).

One notices in each preverbial poem that there are turnings; insinuations grasping like a tendril twisting in its trajectory as it grows toward the light. The reader travels through this poetry like a person wandering in the desert, on high alert for the coiled reptile; yet one also follows the instincts and moves out across the syntactic edges. What becomes voiced here is the lingual/cerebral process of "cutting through"; the reader walks across these terrains scanning the lines as one might scan the night sky.

Within the pages of *Not Even Rabbits Go Down This Hole,* some preverbs echo like daybook entries; we float along in the cloudscapes of Quasha's ever shifting consciousness. "It requires tuning in to the ready to tune" (207). The wisdom that comes through the lines is both bodied and disembodied, arcing across the liminal shifts. There's a substrate of rhythm and tempo to each poem, the language spare and adjectively stripped down. There are lines that seem to come from elsewhere, the daemon whispering through entrancing feminine or dakini-like presences. Many of these preverbial poems address an entity (daemon, dakini, co-conspirator) with declarative assertions. Shams of Tabriz as he declares with Rumi throughout his poetry might be a similar point of reference here.

The beauty found in these preverbial lines is that they allow the reader adequate space in which to interpret and reorient her understanding as individual meanings are allowed to become manifest. The poetic lines serve as an archipelago of interwoven fragments and thereby provide a plethora of gnomic utterance. If the poet writes for the unknown reader, Quasha also writes for the reader who might find herself intent upon making discoveries of self throughout these preverbial entities. How else would one "inhabit the cracks" than by furthering the traipse along pathways of self-discovery?

Conceptually, a preverb can also be essentially elusive—is it some synthetic syntactic creature? Is it language served up as a "reality generator"? Quasha tells us that the preverb is an "event of awareness inside of language" (*Awareness Inside Language*).[3] Preverbs are modalities that can "reorient the mind by shifting language conceptions of what language is" ("Pre Gloss," *Glossodelia Attract,* xi). Language, the stuff of a preverb, makes possible the work of poiesis, and so the poem, the preverb, "is a way that language creates reality" ("Pre Text," *Not Even Rabbits,* xiii), thereby forging a synthetic association of elliptical imagery as a portal to the "self-awareness of language knowing its way" ("Pre Text," xi).

Preverbs also depict what comes into focus during a reader's process of absorbing them. One could say a preverb emerges like a shellfish laying down layers of iridescent chemicals within its shell, where substrate and matrix conjoin to fuse the words into a preverbacious entity. Just so might one's consciousness suddenly lock on to a glistening line such as "Veer further" (*Not Even Rabbits Go Down This Hole*, 277), and effect a real shift in awareness. Inner and outer worlds shift around in an interplay of the mind's blurred terrains, where the exterior world actually turns into psychic substance, as self-weaving thoughts pervade the contents inside of awareness.

> I write for the extremes of attention in a possible reader on whom
> depends a future. (135)

[3] George Quasha and Thomas Fink, *Awareness Inside Language* (2018), see below 163; hereinafter cited in text parenthetically.

Poetry returns us to the state of not being sure of what anything is. (118)

A poem is language with undertow. (79)

You might as well say the poem dreams the reader. (4)

Reading this last line sparks a similar insight from Bachelard: "To read poetry is essentially to dream" (*The Poetics of Space*).[4]

The poetic language of George Quasha demonstrates a juxtaposition of *stance* and *possibility* (or what is *com*possible) as distinct forces align and condition each other in axial space. Meanings may then emerge from the tension between them. One looks outside the window and wonders: Does the axial principle *generate* force, with its tension and compression paradoxically *forcing* an apriori inevitability? What does emerge, as one immerses oneself in the ever-evolving poetic process, is "the ear-mind" working through what Quasha calls "dowsing," with the pen serving as a witching rod, and the ear-mind and pen as conduits to "unknown attractors." A preverb could also be thought of as an inflection moment, as language "thinks through us," and the poem becomes "evolutionary." Preverbial poetry is a process impregnated with the uncertainty principle. This is why Quasha insists that this is the teacher if one becomes resonant with the process.

Poetry is fundamentally essential to the core of our humanity; to sustain this poetic core, then, we should read the texts of poets the way outlaws ride the ridges—scanning the terrain below, with reins held slack for freedom to roam. Preverbial space is essentially the space of irony and paradox, where disorienting moments themselves compose the map while one is busy losing one's way. "The only reliable map is the one you are making while lost" (*Not Even Rabbits,* 104). This brings us to the event horizon of the Rabbit Hole.

What is the nature of this Rabbit Hole anyway? Is it the reality of uncertainty that pervades our moments of not-knowing? One proceeds

---

[4] Gaston Bachelard, *The Poetics of Space* (Boston: Beacon Press, 1969), 17; hereinafter cited in text parenthetically.

through the *terra incognita* of the mind, with intrepid steps crossing vast terrains of unknowing in hope, moving through strange and alien flora, reference points shifting. Space becomes compressed time, cloaking the walker whose eyes are cast against the fiery hues of an evening sky, perhaps serving as the portal to the Infinite. We can't assume there will be some map to project our life by, however; and Quasha has words for us: "Get lost" (238). But proceed intrepidly while doing so! It also seems that uncertainty carries its own traction; perhaps this is one reason why "Poetry makes certainty undesirable" (238). Preverbs are themselves embedded within uncertain spheres of self-discovery as we traverse the process of poiesis. However, we must

> Watch for the hole even rabbits won't go down. (212)

In "The phenomenology of nowhere yet here" (242), what is the relation between the rabbit hole and the "nowhere yet here"? Does it obtain when we enter poetic space in an experience that may have "a high WQ (weirdness quotient)" (25), in that we are actually dreaming with eyes open, as we travel a "long way down" (as in down the rabbit hole), since "uncertainty never goes away" (243)? The insecure way *is* the rabbit hole; and yet the insecure way might actually be the secure way as we spin around the edge of this hole. Poetic evolution happens at the edges, in foldings and unfoldings of axial force. Poetry cuts through *the statis quo* and will always be a synthesizing force. The multiverse turns out to be not just feral … it's also fully conscious!

Here is a phenomenological zoom-in: an interpretative moment, when cream is poured into a cup of black coffee; a swirl, then a dragon appears. As the drinker concentrates on the creamy image, a state of heightened awareness kicks in. Quasha calls this a "spacing into" experience, a "conscious liminality"—the seeing-by-gazing into what is viewed; in this instance, a dragon. But just to cover himself, he addresses the cup's contents: "I apologize to my coffee for missing her creamy swirl, mother of dragons" (43).

Bachelard says it is through reverie that we learn how to do phenomenology.[5] What becomes phenomenologically realized through reading Quasha's unfolding lines is a "penumbral ontology"—that is, one that bites its way into and through the world. When one is open to the wonder of being, say, as the evening melts into its coagulated opacity, the brain sees the gloaming as a "crack between worlds," the day's detritus leaving behind its echoes of dying light. "To notice this space is to find another *there* right there between" (160): in other words, *the phenomenology of beforehand.*

> I keep trying to say there's never enough nothing. (142)

This refers us back to Norman O. Brown's *Love's Body*:

> Get the nothingness back into words. The aim is words with nothing to them; words that point beyond themselves rather than to themselves; transparencies, empty words … corresponding to the void in things.[6]

As the "reverie revs" (*Not Even Rabbits*, 118), the poetic warrior proceeds by putting "pen to paper to draw blood" (87). The pen of the poet is deadly serious; it goes for the visceral.

The preverbial process might be viewed as more than a random traipse, the peripheries scanned with a conscious intent to evolve: "Poetry teaches me I'm an experimental person" (73). The preverbacious configurations, especially in *Not Even Rabbits Go Down This Hole* (like Quasha's previous volumes of preverbs), emulate a reversal strategy that Blake used for shaping the declarative "Proverbs of Hell." What is met *inside* of poetic language (as awareness emerges from the reading/rereadings of the continuous evolution throughout the preverb series) is the poet's standing alongside the knowings and unknowings found across a continuum of epistemic surprise. It is part of "getting out of our own way" as we tune-in to these offerings.

---

[5] Gaston Bachelard, *The Poetics of Reverie* (Boston: Beacon Press, 1969), 14; hereinafter cited parenthetically.

[6] Norman O. Brown, *Love's Body* (New York: Random House, 1966), 259.

In poetry life is at stake in that death is.

(*Not Even Rabbits,* 240)

The poetic image, in its newness, opens a future to language.

(Bachelard, *The Poetics of Reverie,* 3)

"Ending is unending," *Hilaritas Sublime* (13). One thinks of Joyce's *Wake,* or Valery's line about a poem never being completed. George Quasha's process develops across a steadfast exile in the far western frontier of discursive poiesis. He has completed yet another half dozen volumes of preverbs that await publication, the efforts of two decades of intrepidly composing these poetic modalities of mind. The odyssey thus embarked upon, yielding up its riches of preverbial nuggets, anticipates a lode of Quasha's insight-laden humor and (pre)wisdom, as we participate, as co-conspirators, in his unfolding adventure of iridescent poiesis.

Tamas Panitz

With Every Breath a New Native Tongue: Non-Duality and Preverbial Play

George Quasha's *preverbs*, at the level of the couplet, the line, and within the line, continually shrug off and thwart the configurative habits that keep us from the real, from things as they are. Preverbs frustrate narrative, and even their own sequence: lines that came before now come again altered, and the poem is liable to rearrange itself upon recollection or the turning of the page. The lines themselves don't progress so much as change.

My experience in reading seems consistent with what George Quasha says of *preverbs*, that they are self-generating, and at times his involvement is minimal, mere holding onto the pen.

In "A Word *Before*" with which he prefaces *The Daimon of the Moment*, Quasha writes:

> Personal poetic identity, after all, may well be little more than the site of a single emerging language reality with various determinants [...] And yet these seemingly independent lingual events never stray far from the realization that they exist only by force of a principle of non-separateness and interrelated being [...].[1]

Attending the singularity of one's poetic identity is the realness of the real; attending the order of Apollo is the surging of Dionysus; attending the "ego" we find gnosis. This is an essential and insoluble non-duality, neither aspect of which is mutually exclusive, and whose coexistence we find mutually necessitated. Examples abound. And must be held together with others, such as the next one I am going to point out, not in a figure, but like preverbs, as their varieties of expression shift into prominence, retreat, return, play across the sky. As within a single non-duality, such is the interrelation among several.

[1] "A Word *Before*," *The Daimon of the Moment (preverbs)*, 2015, 1; hereinafter cited in text parenthetically.

Another non-duality, though perhaps it's the same one differently, is at the core of Quasha's playfulness, in the relationship of play to game, though I do not mean to suggest this as particularly distinct from the poet's identity.

While preverbs discourage imposed configurations, and thus insist upon themselves with the peculiar beauty of human acts, still they are deeply playful, and there is in play some hint of game. This "game," however, taken from its context, so to speak, is a game played without the rules but those that the drive to play fashions, rules that play requires, however tenuous or strange.

7 ***self-channeling***

With every breath a new native tongue.

Mouth to mouth rerespiration intermits.
Reading is through.

The subject is waiting in the wings.
I find what is lost when *it's* willing.

This fool is persisting in this folly and not getting wise.
Last to read, last to know. Rereading begins.

The pure lure links to the pure land.
Earth sucks mind effluvia as all flows home.

Saying magnetizes in any language and from one to another.
Who speaks for herself at the crossroads speaks for all.

Mind given her way in the sway's transgender.
It takes one to know one even when it isn't one.

Reading through certain texts confusion sets in and you hear voices.
We know we've entered the impersona's space as the voices are
hearing themselves.

The mind can't be shattered but it turns away from itself.[1]

This is a new game—removed from any game types and game theory, and into meditation, as the game of play itself: and the aim of this play is to engage things as they are. There is the other meaning of game, the attitude of preparedness, "I'm game for whatever," the surrender, to play anything, without putting up resistance. *Being game* the *game of play* manifests: to the poet's receptivity the preverbs organize themselves—that is the poet's power.

The preverbs continue being written and show no signs of stopping. They show no signs of beginning either. The play that I've described precludes such distinctions. Considering the sheer length (some fourteen volumes, seven of which have been published, along with six chapbooks, and recently six preverb-photo collaborations with Susan Quasha) of this ever growing, expansive and singular work, we remember the game of the hunter, game as prey. But this is no commercial hunter of bison or ducks. There is no causal reason, however abstracted, for our hunter, and the game is no more responsible for the hunter's existence than hunger or fear;[2] rather all are tied into a complex ecology, and as with anything endless, or undying, whether preverbs or Lincoln's assassination, we find attached some hint of the eternal.

So, *what game is the hunter after?*

The answer is in the structure of the preverbs themselves. It is found, for example, in the interrelationship of the non-duality of hunter and quarry, each with their own non-dual existence, who turn out to be one

---

1 *The Daimon of the Moment (preverbs)*, 2015, 26; hereinafter cited in text parenthetically.

2 "And the wind said I never knew that wolves could be afraid. The wolf answered, Fear makes language, fear makes us speak. Everything that speaks knows how to be afraid." —from Robert Kelly, *Seven Fairy Tales: The Wind and the Wolf*, available online.

and the same. This is not unlike the living mystery of the Jungian *Mysterium Coniunctionis.*

Our hunter is both "the personal poetic identity," utter singularity, and Being itself, undifferentiated. His game is things themselves, individuals, things as they are; which exist "by the force of a principle of non-separateness and interrelated being." So within the non-duality of hunter and game are crosscurrents.

And yet these non-dualities do not simply resolve their dynamic by being together, but multiply upon inspection. "Hunter" and "game" change their names, genders, and positions, ever complicating the discourse directly about them, as well as the context for discourse: now language, now "reality," philosophy, psychology, etc., exposing the stupidity of exclusivity.

According to Quasha in *Awareness Inside Language* (George Quasha in conversation with Thomas Fink), poems, including preverbs, are composed "in a sort of continuum, one end of which is deliberate construction, by whatever poetic principle, and the other end something like pure and spontaneous inspiration ('received'), whatever that in fact means."[3] Thus one preverb may be radically different or radically similar to another: a preverb can both ask and answer a question as it radically engages the crosscurrents of this "continuum's" poles.

Preverbs are a response to such "impossible but necessary questions," (*Awareness,* 16) as *What game is the hunter after;* and humorously, they might to a degree be the possible and unnecessary answers, or vice versa: the possible and unnecessary question might draw the impossible and necessary answer. There is no end to the combinations, each unique. As Quasha describes them: "Lines ask to be known individually, not because they fit a pattern or are part of a development, narrative, or formal symbolism, but according to the intrinsic event of the line, which is highly variable in rhythm, content, syntax, diction, etc. Everything must speak for itself, without supervening justification" (*Awareness,* 35).

---

[3] George Quasha and Thomas Fink, "'Awareness Inside Language': On George Quasha's Preverbs," www.Jacket2.org (13 May 2016); see below 162.

Chris Funkhouser

Listening as Learning: Documenting *Preverbs*

Starting in Fall 2017, and over many meetings since, I have recorded George Quasha reading his body of poems known as *preverbs*, forming the intention to chronicle the entirety of them up to the present point in time. The following reflections concern the extraordinary experience of instructively collaborating with Quasha as we document his poetry using sound recording equipment.[1]

I

Upon first encountering and reading Quasha's series of poems known as *preverbs*—which, without premeditation, became the focus of our ongoing project together—I had little sense of what these poems actually were or what they represented in terms of poetics. However, listening to an abundance of this work as it was spoken, and again during the editing of my recordings, has given me an opportunity to learn what preverbs are. Initially, I presumed connections between *preverbs* and *proverbs*, not realizing what lines of his work consist of, how they are made or should be approached. I did not think to recognize a bond between p*reverbs* and Quasha's *axial* principles that are reflected throughout his work as an artist—which he has clearly, if sometimes reluctantly, theorized.

The preverbs' basic principles connect with Blake's perception of language as being self-regulating, "a precarious self-balancing of dynamic contraries," and with forces such as *axiality*, as explained in commentaries by Quasha included in some of his volumes such as *Verbal Paradise* (2011) and *Things Done for Themselves* (2015).[2] As a scholar, I had read his explanations, but did not begin to fully understand various principles at play—until I began recording and editing his work.

[1] The ongoing recordings are archived on PennSound after editing: writing.upenn.edu/pennsound/x/Quasha.php.

[2] *Verbal Paradise (preverbs)*, 2001, vii; *Things Done for Themselves (preverbs)*, 2015; hereinafter cited in text parenthetically.

A year earlier (Summer 2016), I participated in the Robert Kelly Study Group's community reading of preverbs. Event performers received advance instructions for "unpreparing" for the reading, composed by Charles Stein; yet my presentation from Quasha's poems was done improperly. (I read an excerpt from *Things Done for Themselves*.) Ignoring Stein's observation that preverbs "cannot in principle be rehearsed" and that "we not try too hard to prepare ourselves to read these pieces," I rehearsed, essentially using a basic approach—that is, delivering lines in a single breath, using punctuation marks as breathing points—which is not the most principled way to read these lines. Stein also had mentioned—quite rightly, though I had not grasped its implications at the time—how "what distinguishes this work is that it depends in a remarkable way on the concrete events/acts of reading them, in the very moment that these occur."[3] Conversing during one of our early recording sessions, as I began grasping certain nuances within the preverbs, Quasha strikingly declared, "each line has its own poetics."

One of the facts about his performance in reading preverbs is that he treats every line as if seeing it for the first time. The language itself remains fixed via the page, yet a line's vocal rendering is spontaneous and variable, depending on how it is perceived in the moment of reading. At first, I felt that Quasha, in cultivating this characteristic of the work, was making the process of reading more difficult than necessary—particularly as such a method of verbal registration leads to dozens of lines that require re-recording in a documentary setting. Yet learning of, and observing, his on-the-fly recitation practices, as we pursued our collaborative recording project, has helped me to appreciate and understand Quasha's poetics much more than I would have done otherwise.

At the group preverbs reading, I wished I had had a more refined approach to forming the delivery of lines, divining meaning by voice in the moment, taking on the challenge of such a chore much as the author does. I would never again read preverbs aloud as I did on that occasion. A singular "correct" processual approach to reading or reciting these poems is never imposed by Quasha, however, so my being aware of this

[3] Email to author (July 10, 2016).

type of inside knowledge may not be crucial to engaging with the work. Nonetheless, to listen to Quasha read, one must be aware that he starts each line from scratch. Although he revisits the work before recording sessions—familiarizing himself with the lines—he conceives his delivery of them on the spot.

The process I experience in watching and recording Quasha indeed reflects a comment that appears in *The Daimon of the Moment* (2015): "I could say," he writes, that a "*preverb* appears as one-line utterance projecting a particular state of language in the act of finding itself here and now" (134)[4]. In an email following our earliest sessions, he writes:

> While a principle of preverbs is that there can be any number of 'right' readings of a line/poem, there is an issue for me of getting the voice to not just perform well but what I call *self-truly*. This becomes performative in the [J.L.] Austin sense of performativity. When I was doing the reading, I experienced most of the reading to be in fact self-true, so I'm happy from that perspective.[5]

Having previewed *The Daimon of the Moment*, and other books in which he offers explanations of preverbs, I should have had more of a preconception of what producing recordings of these poems with Quasha might entail. He considers his writing of preverbs, in *Daimon of the Moment*, "a precarious language act, an event at an edge that remains on edge in the reading," which includes "excitable language showing up as one-liner and intentionally inviting configurative reading" (134-35). In *Things Done for Themselves*, Quasha describes the preverb as "a one-line intentional act of language that invites configurative reading as a singular event of meaning" (177). Though I had familiarized myself with this contextual framework in advance, I did not realize the full implications of how Quasha's "*axial principle in language*" made meaning out of "an intense and present act of choice or perhaps spontaneous insight, with the awareness that any construction thereof is impermanent" (*Daimon*

---

[4] *The Daimon of the Moment (preverbs)*, 2015, 134; hereinafter cited in text parenthetically.

[5] Email to author (November 1, 2017).

134). Thus the lines Quasha reads will sometimes topple over themselves along the way. When this occurs, we pause and the line is reread, until errors, as it were, are absent. As I have indicated, our first sessions together struck me by the manner in which they divulged how Quasha's axial delivery process leads to many *mistakes* when he reads (which are not difficult to correct). I confided my view that his process made reading poems more difficult than necessary and then learned why.

For my own convenience in editing audio files for public presentation, I carefully notate in margins of a text every time Quasha makes such a mistake in delivery, so that I may more easily remove the errors using software (which, for this part of the production, has been Adobe Audition). My copies of *Glossodelia Attract*[6] and *The Daimon of the Moment* show more than one hundred twenty edits that were needed to be made to the files for the two books. Working with the books as production scripts, as well as artifacts, is useful for many reasons, not the least of which is that they are a convenient way to register my responses to hearing the poems.

Marginalia in my copies of these volumes include passages highlighted with stars, underlines, exclamation points, smiley faces, and other notations that may have, for example, indicated where a printed word was unintentionally replaced by another. A digital scan of a poem from *The Daimon of the Moment* (shown below) illustrates some of these annotations; these are my immediate responses to hearing the poems, and they track where edits were needed to be made in the audio files. The book itself becomes an object capturing my experience and engagement with hearing Quasha read, all of which makes me wonder how many readers read along with books, as they listen to recordings—a practice I find valuable not only because I hear the voice, but also because I consider an author's speed of delivery (including dramatic pauses), gaining a better understanding of my practices as a reader.

---

[6] *Glossodelia Attract (preverbs)*, 2015; hereinafter cited in text parenthetically.

9 ***you'll never walk alone or long on an edge***

Here's how it works: it tells me nothing till it hits me in the face.
Don't ask me what I believe because it's a bad question.

The language construct is a variable free space with secret chaotic desires.
What is this attraction to life over the edge?

This is how it talks to itself.
Through inhabited disorientation seeing in configurative depth is restorative.

We need a long life those of us who touch promised land on the sly or the fly.
Gender contender I read back on through in speaking of her from within.

<cough>

A poem motivates my Doubting Thomas to keep an eye on syntax slipping away.
It's never enough to say without being said.

read faster (sometimes much) than I've voiced the lines

Lazy syntax is a leak in the music.
Getting dizzy on the issue is a high.

I forget when I come down.
My cloud rains on my parade.

Ever since the fateful night light reality comes instantly across its threshold.
Saturated meaning bellows.

We are left saying what has never been and can scarcely be, before now.

alternatives to itself

like proverbs, but private (spoken presentation) which can shift meaning

28

Page 28 from The Daimon of the Moment *with Chris Funkhouser recording notes*

At the left margin (above), a marked line indicates where Quasha needed to repeat, and therefore where I also needed to cut from the session's audio file. A bracketed "<cough>" notation pinpoints where another edit should be made in the final version of the sound document. Some personal notes to myself appear, one mentioning that I read "faster (sometimes much) than he voices the lines," a detail which may not be significant, inasmuch as it may be fair to presume most people read faster than they experience language when they listen to it. At the bottom of the page, I am drawing comparison between proverbs and preverbs, noting the latter features "variable spoken presentation, which can shift meaning—alternatives to itself." Reflected here is how I am directly absorbing a significant distinction between proverb and preverb. Many pages of books and manuscripts we have recorded contain such production information, as well as received understandings regarding Quasha's poetics. Whether or not they are useful to anyone else, registering the direct connection between voice, text, and listening experience, helps me embrace what transpires during our sessions. These notes help me remember what seemed important in the moment.

Beginning to make recordings of Quasha's work in 2017, an overall projection, of course, did not yet exist. We discussed the project in advance, and I asked him to select works he wished to record, but we had no particular long-range view. After our first round of sessions (October 2017 - January 2018), which are now the foundation of Quasha's PennSound webpage, I realized what my goal would be: to record every preverb that Quasha has written. Thus far, using Ableton Live software, Quasha and I have recorded four complete volumes of preverbs (*Verbal Paradise, Glossodelia Attract, The Daimon of the Moment,* and *Things Done for Themselves*) and six series, some published as print or online chapbooks (*The Ghost In Between, Scorned Beauty Comes Up From Behind, Hearing Other, Polypoikilos: matrix in variance, The First House/Every Sound Its Word* and *Not Even Rabbits Go Down This Hole* [the full volume of the same name containing this series and "The First House"... has subsequently been published but are so far unrecorded]);[7]

[7] Along with the books *Verbal Paradise, Glossodelia Attract, The Daimon of the*

these publications represent about half of the preverbs work to date (as of this writing)—fourteen books of which seven are in print. We proceed, envisioning this body of writings as a long-term endeavor.

Our recording project is itself axial in that it is "*free* being," without any type of established timeline in constructing a preverbs archive.[8] Given the many demands we have on our respective lives, this component of the collaboration is especially welcome. At the outset I did not anticipate that recording Quasha would become such an extraordinary task and large-scale project, but, once I began hearing the collections of preverbs, I became enthralled by their complexity and Quasha's aesthetic intentions in composing, organizing, and producing these works. In our twenty-three hours or so of recording we have only covered approximately a fifth of the preverbs (roughly 12,000 of 50,000-70,000 lines). With still a long way to go, my perspective on the poems has gained considerable depth.

Among the steady transmissions that appear throughout the preverbs is Quasha's direct address of *poiesis* or what, through his lens, poetry is. Early on in our sessions, I realized that in preverbs Quasha often addresses the matter of poetry's multiple identities. Several lines in each of the books we recorded begin with a kind of self-reflexive phrase, "Poetry is…," alternatively stated as "Language is…," "The poem…," or "Poems…." When I pointed this characteristic out to him, he said he was unaware of the habit. Pursuing the matter, to further amplify Quasha's sense of openness and comprehension of both authority and form, as I was preparing for a performance in New York, in December 2017, I spliced together a number of the "Poetry is…" lines from the preverbs, in order to play them over loudspeakers during my reading. Most Serene Congress, an improvisational music ensemble I work with, added

---

Moment, and *Things Done for Themselves*, the six chapbooks are as follows. *The Ghost In Between*, 2018; *Scorned Beauty Comes Up From Behind*, 2012; *Hearing Other*, 2018; *Polypoikilos: matrix in variance*, 2017; *The First House/Every Sound Its Word*, 2018; and *Not Even Rabbits Go Down This Hole*, 2018 (the full volume of the same name containing this series and *The First House*, 2020).

[8] Cf. George Quasha, *Axial Stones: An Art of Precarious Balance*, foreword, Carter Ratcliff, 20.

a musical soundtrack to the piece (which interested readers can hear via our Soundcloud webpage). This recording makes vivid the variability and vocal energy with which Quasha delivers his lines. It discloses a focused, if unintentional, passion on the subject.

The undefinable meaning of poetry is of distinct interest to Quasha. Another of his major projects is a series of art videos with documentary value titled *poetry is* (together with videos titled, respectively, *art is* and *music is*).[9] Since 2002, Quasha has interviewed on video more than a thousand poets, artists and musicians in eleven countries, asking each person to offer their own perspective on the relevant one of the three topics. The range of artists featured in these videos, along with the diversity of answers received from his questions, proves how unpindownable his three topics and his own forms are.[10]

II

Thus far I have outlined some of the logistical facts of production, indicating compelling, educational aspects of working with Quasha's preverbs. Other driving, if not profound, dimensions exist. Beyond recording, handling, and preserving the data I have discussed, I want to add that I have experienced what I can only describe as a *ritual* in my technical preparations for working with Quasha.

I enter an octagonal room in his home in Barrytown (negotiating its built-in sounds), where we assemble audio equipment and create our sound files. (In addition, Quasha makes videos of our sessions, for himself.) We work together to make something gratifying happen. Sitting in a room, with another person, for an hour or two, memorializing poems is something I am very familiar with at this point. I value the experience. Yet it is still an odd and unusual activity—its glories and awkwardnesses are somewhat hard to describe.

---

[9] George Quasha, et al. *poetry is, art is, music is,* all three available online.

[10] Excerpts from the video have also appeared in print form, via a book edited by Quasha titled *art is (Speaking Portraits)* (New York: PAJ Publications, 2016), which features still images and transcribed quotations taken from the video footage. The videos are viewable online at art-is-international.org.

Several weeks after we began our project, I received an email from Quasha in which he explained some of why he appreciated the project. I felt a resonance with my own creative values, instincts, and practices in working on elaborate documentary media productions in the past. Beyond graciously expressing gratitude for my effort, he made a particularly salient point, one that addresses the benefits of a focused collaboration of the type and duration we were engaged in:

> Thanks for doing the work with me. What you're doing is important on many levels, perhaps the least obvious is the contribution this kind of attention makes to poet-psychesphere—the shared mind space that valorizes poetic mind. We depend on that in many ways, mostly unacknowledged. Most of the time we may not even acknowledge that it exists—the shared dimension of creative mind. But it's there and it's vitally important. It's not about culture, though culture preserves it (when it does—it can also destroy). We do what we can to sustain it. It's about feeding the conscious engagement—and there's an element of *prajna* in it (for those who understand that level).[11]

Most poets do see the importance in recording/documenting their work and broadcasting it more widely. The rest of Quasha's missive addresses a profound point that took me years to realize: through specifically this type of documentary work, a unique intimacy develops. The "poet-psychesphere," as he writes, is something I have experienced many times over the decades; and, importantly, while it may be as ephemeral as anything else, our having had such a "shared mind space" has evolved into something more deeply human and lasting.

Quasha's email invokes the Buddhist concept of *prajna*, which succinctly comports with my own drive, purpose, and meaning I have derived from extended media practice. *Prajna* may be baldly defined as *wisdom*, though the concept, in its essence, contains much more depth. The level of insight (into reality) indicated by *prajna* is built upon recognition of impermanence, suffering, non-self, and emptiness. Making

---

[11] Email to author (November 14, 2017).

recordings for archival and other purposes aspires to preserve voices and other sounds, yet it seems unlikely that media in any format will have a long shelf-life. Practices such as mine cannot be said to have created or caused significant suffering; certain degrees of aggravation, however, difficulty and despair occasionally arise.

In the present era, documentary work is done by someone who sits in the background, away from the microphone, with some digital hardware. Audio experiments are conducted, if for nothing else, in order to devise and add to alternative approaches to the treatment of language that can be presented to be heard. Large-scale organizational operations benefit from having groups of people who, collaboratively, make an effort to achieve a common end. One discovers many contemplative aspects within such self-motivated, yet often selfless, work. Acts of recording, sound design, performance, and audio production eventually become a form of meditation that delivers insight. Through such practice I have gained insight more broadly into literature, communication, cooperation, and trust in intuition.

On another occasion, I received this most generous, valuable email transmission from Quasha. It speaks directly to a range of concerns I better understand now are relevant to our relationship:

> It's been a strong experience reading the preverbs aloud over the past weeks—I guess we've now done some 12 hours of recording sessions and the same number of "series" of preverbs. Reading aloud at length and over extended time (as the two-hour sessions, which can be somewhat challenging, and as the extension over weeks) brings forward a larger experience that, in my sense of it, is close to the nature of the work, and at the same time rather tricky to characterize. For instance, it brings forward the spatial textscape, in the sense of the extent of text as a field of resonance—as though the whole "poem" comprises all series in all the books and any given point (or line) relates to all others. It clarifies that the poem tends to educate reading (appropriate to it) by way of engaging listening. A core tenet of poetics for me is that poetry invents ways of reading. And it also invents ways of listening which feed back into ways of

reading—and ultimately ways of writing (esp. as generating poetry). It opens listening to conscious and unconscious connections in the full body of the work, as resonances of what has been heard previously coming into what is being heard at a given moment.

This puts the reader somewhat in the space of the poet—access to a "poetic world" or a dimension characterized by its own language. And thinking this puts me in mind of a principle appropriate to this work: that one has to learn a poet's language, in a sense not so different from learning a foreign language. The fact that it happens in "one's own" language obscures how different one's actual own language (an idiolect) is from that of others, since we tend to emphasize similarities in the interest of communicating and establishing commonality. Poetry that seems difficult or odd or somehow disruptive of understanding calls forward the idiolectual dimension. And listening makes very immediate this problematic in ways that are particularly instructive in a poetics.

Listening differs from reading, for instance, by bypassing the pause-reflect-compare access of the page/screen-held textual reading—you can't go back. (Of course editing, like what you're doing, returns to something more like text, and in any case you follow the reading text-in-hand.) Yet as literate listeners we are still aware that there is a "back there"—a back that is now afield, accessible mainly through quick memory and resonance. So, the ear's resorting to its own discriminatory power opens a certain direct receptivity—of being spoken *to*. The agree/disagree function is softened and different levels of receptivity are activated, both consciously and unconsciously. It seems that being reader-listener is closer to the condition of poet "riding on ears." (E.g., what Duncan called, after Pound, "the tone-leading of vowels.") What I would call the "penetration quotient" is altered—what gets in, how far, to what effect. It's a cut below rationalist discrimination, with the effect of activating aural imagination.

We're in a domain here of the phenomenology of listening and how it's distinct, though not entirely, from that of reading. Listening to poetry overlaps the writing-speaking that generates it. In reading the poems aloud I also engage listening, even as I get in touch with the writing-speaking that created it. I'm also at the same time reading a text and so become more acutely aware of how speaking/listening creates an instantly new version, itself an idiolect, a singularity. In the case of preverbs this folds back into the "amphibolous message" of the text—its opportunity for variable in-process reflective reading-listening. A session of reading aloud renews the text for me—an energetic trajectory that no doubt carries over into further composition (usually the same night). This emphasizes how complexly the performance of poetry is complicit with the continuing life of making poetry. How this plays out in the social context of poetry is infinitely complex and mostly impossible to track. A difficulty there is that we think in terms of "influence" in a way that is far too simplistic relative to the actual phenomenon. For instance, matters of "style" and the like may play little or no role in what is actually transmitted. I've long felt that, as important as direct influence can be, a better model for what one poet gives another is "transmission." But this calls into play certain understandings of mind that are not easily introduced into literary discussion.

What could be called "expanded field of listening," for what occurs in longer sessions over time, can engage an experience of what I call *meeting thoughts from afar.* It has to do with emergent language of obscure origin—one feels it in the mind as something different from ordinary thinking. Over the years I've cultivated a particularly subtle version of this. I suppose it's related to other histories such as "automatic writing" and "channeling" but for me these overstate the case, make it seem dramatic. For me it's subtle and interconnected with one's conscious thinking—yet it's also quite distinctively itself. The thinking here suggests that the

> expanded field of listening is a sort of mimesis of *meeting thoughts from afar*. The field resonance should open receptivity to subtle emergent insight inside language. I would say that that's a core intention of axial poetics.
>
> This is meant to let you know how the experience of recording preverbs has been important to me.[12]

III

Collegiality aside, Quasha's message highlights a number of potentially valuable outcomes from our recording project. Human interactions that involve "engaged listening" are a rarity, and we are in a situation where we need to invent and manifest "ways of listening"—which for me has evolved into cultivating *instructive* ways of listening. I value the entering into a "poetic world" in such a way, having the experience and instruction "of being spoken *to*." Having worked on several extensive single-author recording projects, Quasha's sense of an "expanded field of listening" agrees with me.[13] I experience an informative, genuine, human outcome while being stimulated by sophisticated, wise literary creations and perspectives. If I hadn't realized the preverbs' thoughtful underpinnings, their "opportunity for variable in-process reflective reading-listening" (cf. above), I certainly was well-aware of their capacities by this juncture.

As Quasha says, in one of the preverbs from *Glossodelia Attract*, "My work is not experimental, I am" (72). His active engagement of Eastern spirituality—over the course of nearly a half-century, including t'ai chi, meditation, and healing arts—sets him apart from most everyone else I come into contact with, and informs his poetics in most interesting ways. Like the preverbs, Quasha embodies openness regarding his own diverse nature.

---

[12] Email to author (December 8, 2017).

[13] Other projects of mine have included collaborating with Peter Lamborn Wilson and Charles Stein, for instance, including on their respective author pages at PennSound, and with Andy Clausen on Audible.

To be sure, apart from matters I have already discussed, there is to be had an understanding of how the carefully phrased swoosh of language in his lines, the effect of it, expressively parallels the experience of his axial paintings. The overall trans-medial unity in his work more than interests me. Despite their differences in form, the fluidity of his poetic language is so very like the swerves of paint he creates instantaneously, purely intuitively, in his axial paintings. It is particularly in this sense that he is a trans-medial artist whose in-the-moment compositional approach pulls into a unity different strands of his work. I am impressed by how much energy his demanding approach adds to the output.

"Overall, I see lack of authoritative modeling as a positive fact in poetry," Quasha has written in an essay of his he titled "Healing Poetics," which sets out his praxis, "not only for the good of diversity," he continues, "but for the trust it encourages in conscious poetic process itself. No doubt we would have to betray poetry to pin it down" (*Poetry in Principle* 34). Reciting his preverbs, Quasha isn't simply going through the motions of reading a text he has previously read and perfected. Rather, his effort is to make each line a new experience for himself—through which a unique vibrancy is transmitted, in each poem. This is a powerful experience to be present for, to receive the communication.

The relevance of his remark, "Tape recorder joins typewriter as instrumentation of the muse,"[14] which I uncovered forty years later, is even greater, more salient now, possibly more than ever. It rings in a most valuable potentiality—one of wide-ranging benefit given the portability of our technologies. As someone who has an exorbitant amount of direct experience with sound recording and audio production, I concur with his prescient observation, while I am inclined to add that the recorder is not only potentially a muse; it is also a most valuable, instructive tool.

Listening to poetry, in many cases, slows down the process of reception, which opens the possibility of more time to think inside the

---

[14] In Quasha's 1977 essay "Dialogos: Between the Written and the Oral in Contemporary Poetry" (*New Literary History* 8: 488, 1977); reprinted in Jerome Rothenberg and Diane Rothenberg, eds. *Symposium of the Whole: A Range of Discourse Toward an Ethnopoetics,* 461-74 (Berkeley: University of California Press, 1983).

formations of language, what is being said and done there—and the particular experience of the poem as a listener receives it. The first-hand experience of hearing a poet's voice traverse the course of a book (in Quasha's case a series of books) instructs and inspires me as much as, if not more than, reading the work on the page.

Rhinebeck, New York
July 2019

Chris Funkhouser recording George Quasha reading preverbs for PennSound archive (2017)

Thomas Fink

In Conversation with George Quasha

Awareness Inside Language[1]

Note: *After reading several of George Quasha's collections of "preverb" poems with great interest, I was intrigued by his development of this new poetic mode, the way it shaped the organization of his work over a substantial period of time and the persistent metapoetic (even metalinguistic) thrust of the poetry. George kindly consented to engage in an exchange, and we limited the discussion to four of his preverb books. The interview took place via email from January 8 to February 23, 2016*

The four books under consideration are:

Verbal Paradise (preverbs), 2011
Glossodelia Attract (preverbs), 2015
Things Done for Themselves (preverbs), 2015
The Daimon of the Moment (preverbs), 2016

Thomas Fink: In the "Pre Play" to *Verbal Paradise*, you refer to the preverb as a "kledomantic gathering of stray language according to a singularity-centered principle of organization" (x) and go on to say that these enactments of singularity work "for the public good" by promoting "the destabilization of naming" (ix), which is valuable in a culture that names things and concepts too simply and often coercively. I couldn't find the word "kledomantic" anywhere, but I think that this notion of destabilization is familiar to those who have been involved with the reading and/

[1] This conversation first appeared in *Jacket2* as "Awareness Inside Language: On George Quasha's preverbs" (May 13, 2016; online), and subsequently was reprinted in short interim editions series of poetics thinking as *Matrices #1* (Barrytown, NY: Station Hill Press, 2018).

or writing of innovative poetry; in "pre gnoetic," which is placed after the preverb poems of *The Daimon of the Moment*, you write: "The role of poetry is to do what language can't, or won't, otherwise do" (132). You identify the preverb as a "one-line utterance projecting a particular state of language in the act of finding itself here and now" (134). Like the proverb—we will get to your precursor Blake later—a preverb honors "the impulse to *say* what's true" but also evades "the inevitable limitation of thinking one knows the truth" (134). Let's take five examples of metacognitive utterances to put flesh on these abstractions:

> The truth eats its own. (*Verbal Paradise*, 11)

> There's a meaning between assertions the poem can hardly escape. (*Verbal Paradise*, 34)

> Language cannot respond to inquiry into its nature without feedback from you. (*Glossodelia Attract*, 63)

> This meditation on meditation as reading is not premeditated. (*Things Done for Themselves*, 11)

> It is not the function of language to say what is true. (*The Daimon of the Moment*, 12)

In the first and fifth of the preverbs above, you seem to be positing the truth of limitation itself or limitation of the presumption of truth as (negative?) truth. In the second one, you posit the existence of truth as meaning, but only "between assertions" in a poem, and thus you entertain the speaking/writing subject's possible inability to put that in-between truth into words. In the third preverb, you suggest that metalinguistic truth cannot exist outside of the limitations of individual subjectivity. And the emphasis on lack of premeditation in your meta-meditations indicates that contingency structures the possibilities of truth-effects, thus also questioning the accessibility of (universal, atemporal) "Truth."

I'm aware that my repeated use of the pronoun "you" just now may ascribe a unity of your self and the implied speaker(s) of the preverbs, and that may not be your intention.

I'd love to learn what "kledomantic" might signify, but more importantly, how do you as author/reader of the preverbs above align the play of truth-seeking/awareness of limitation (articulated in the prose of "Pre Gnoetic") with the thematic dynamics of the actual preverbs?

George Quasha: Thank you for inquiring in a way that allows me to focus on the actual way that preverbs work, which you do by interestingly posing in effect a question-complex with many elements. As such it asks for a like response, an equivalent complex—which is, like the poems or poem-complexes that preverbs form in and beyond the books you mention, not so much non-linear (since we inevitably follow a time-line of some kind in language) as multi-linear—many lines doing many things with their own timing. So, at the onset I have to specify two principles: 1) The axiality of linearity, meaning that every line of thought we may follow has its own axis and turns thought in its own way, which may or may not be consistent with other lines of thought running alongside; consequently, at no point are we building a case in the logical sense but only gathering perspectives and exploring together. 2) The presumption of authorship is itself complex and always in some degree unattested or quasi-attested or ambiguously attested. In short, the nature of authorship is always in question, and the self-reflective nature of the poetic process inevitably thematizes this quest—not, that is, x-characters in search of an author as in the theater frame, but n-texts inquiring into authorship in its nature. All the balls are in the air and if one hits ground it bounces back up.

You acknowledge the second point in mentioning the problematic "you," and of course I'm doing the answering, me as me. But this discourse is not the poem, and I do not represent the poem nor the poem me, because the poetic domain sensitive to *axiality*—let's define the axial for the moment as *radical variability*, variability to the root of the thought—is *linguality*, language reality or language as reality-generator. Poetics is the effort we make to track that generative process and apply it to the thinking we do in any other context. This is not an "art for art's sake" approach since the notion of art or poetry is itself variable, unstable and in question at every point; and the very notion of "for the sake of" is variable. (Nor is it "language poetry" since I'm not part of that historical event directly, and, although I appreciate that phenomenon and enjoy the work of the poets who identify with it, I have for very fundamental reasons chosen to create my own terminology and poetics with no social agreement or authorization as such. Consistency of thought is not inherently virtuous in this approach.) But, as anything I may say is at best perspectival, I am not the authority on the meaning and import of preverbs. They speak for themselves, and I enjoy the process of engaging in their radial effect. I experience them as instructive of my thinking.

I should also say that the question of authorship is conditioned by the process by which preverbs come to be. And addressing this briefly may help with how we think together about preverbs. I do not construct them, and a constructivist theory is inadequate for their nature. I could say I "receive" them but that would imply a sender, which I can't verify or know, even though in certain moments and moods it definitely feels like they're coming from elsewhere. They weave through the kind of thinking I seem to do in response to other thinking/reading, but a preverb comes to be when I feel it happening of its own accord in the mind *and* in the body. I think Robert Duncan said something like that—a certain body tone says the poem is happening, and you follow ("a search in obedience"). I consider that I have about thirty seconds to write it down before it evaporates—and I've lost many through carelessness, not having my notebook to hand, or thinking that it's so vivid that I'll never forget it and of course do; then it haunts me like a dream and I spend hours off and on trying to recall it, and in a sense grieving. They have the strange quality of seeming both mine and wholly other. At times I've thought that they must be somewhat related to the Surrealist practice of automatic writing, but the descriptions of that phenomenon are not like my experience with preverbs, and the sort of wild combination of scarcely related objects has a very different feel from what shows up in preverbs. Likewise my old friend Hannah Weiner's seeing words on your forehead which she'd tell you on the spot! Preverbs seem to want to stay within possible syntactic bounds (inviting thought to try them on), which they violate, perhaps becoming paratactic, through internal multiplicity—more "rule" extension than avoidance.

Let me engage your thinking to guide my own further thought here:

The truth eats its own.

You say (I translate your "you" to "it"), it seems "to be positing the truth of limitation itself or limitation of the presumption of truth as (negative?) truth." Preverbs engage logic(s) but they never actually "posit" anything, since there's no evident intention to *claim* truth or untruth or even the limitation of truth. Everything is limited and potentially unlimited, or limited until proving unlimited *in one's own mind as reader.* You understand "The truth eats its own" as "positing the truth of limitation itself" etc. which is how it configures in your reading; that's neither right nor wrong as such, but it's interesting to think and contributes to further positioning of (the notion) truth in the mind. The preverb, however, is not doing that; you are. In the preverb truth is eating its own, which when read is configurative however that comes about. I could read it as an "image" of Saturn eating his children (I don't, but I could). I could think, truth can't be fixed because whatever seems true is devoured by its own process of furthering or by life taking it into its digestive system. These are configurations inspired by the preverb. And one formulation that often comes up in my thinking is that preverbs are configurative, just as I say *axial drawings* (on the front covers of all four books of preverbs) are neither figurative nor abstract but configurative. That describes the *optional nature of interpretative viewing.* Axial poems like axial drawings inspire configurative response, which is a *singularity* in the experience of the reader/viewer. We appreciate abstract "form" and we tend to see "figures" or something of both and that's configuration. Axial language creates the opportunity to engage that freedom of configuration within the terms appropriate to the mind at that time. I tend to think that exercising that kind of "freedom" grows something intrinsic to mind and allows language reality to be the site of uncorrupted life process, and even makes possible a world very different from the corrupt one we live in. That's one of my favorite configurations.

The above discussion could be viewed as a process generated by the preverb: *It is not the function of language to say what is true.* That of course plays against the Liar's Paradox ("This is a lie"), and its contrary is equally (un)true. But it's not any one thing and not a game of logical burlesque. It engages actual thinking processes and allows their formulations to live through the very limitations they discover—to "further process" the thinking in a field of language larger than the limitations, perhaps I could say, more open to *lingual psychonautics.*

You ask about *kledomantic,* which is the adjective of *kledomancy,* "divination by keys" understood sometimes as "oracular interpretation of stray remarks," a practice that goes back to ancient times, such as sitting in a room of many people talking and allowing the intersection of phrases to create coherent patterns; it may be viewed as embracing synchronicity. (The ancient Oracle did not make better sense than that; the burden of interpretation is on the listener.) Gertrude Stein is said to have practiced something akin. One could understand this as "chance" in a sense related to the various ways Jackson Mac Low worked—accepting the incursion of language as *guided from within.* And here I have to note that preverbs do not accept the categories "subjective" and "objective," which are reductive almost to the point of uselessness. The "limitation" of "truth" is not mainly a problematic of subjectivity or its opposition to objectivity; neither animal roams the preverbial forest for more than a moment. Language is itself an intersection of "interior" and "exterior," mine and the world's, personal and impersonal, etc. Its nature is radically open. The discipline of preverbs is to remain true to that actual complexity. I sometimes think of Stevens' "The accuracy of accurate letters is an accuracy with respect to the structure of reality."

The above discussion could be a gloss on *There's a meaning between assertions the poem can hardly escape.* Assertion is not the only site of meaning; there are other orders of meaning not discovered by language as assertion or any other familiar "mood." It depends in part on context. And on *level,* in the sense, say, that Newtonian physics is an adequate tool for a mechanical problem but not for a subatomic one. Preverbs extend the permission of poetry to shift levels at any point, indeed continuously as the actual experience of mind does throughout any given 24 hour period. (In this frame a preverb could contain a 24-hour dynamic condensed to under a quarter minute.)

Language cannot respond to inquiry into its nature without feedback from you. There is no language without person; language uses us to journey through its own nature; beings originate (to invoke Buddha's idea) interdependently; life itself is sustained by feedback process which language serves—these are some configurations of the above preverb. You register it in relation to metalinguistics, which is an option that considers the objectification of community in relation to language; at times I follow a related (proto-Bakhtinian) path of thinking. Equally reasonable is a biodynamic dimension: feedback, energy, physical connection between speech act and bodymind, proprioception, and so on. Another perspective is *language is alive and self-generative* in relation to mind activity. We say that we think in language, but we could just as easily say that language thinks in us or through us. In that view poetry does the "higher" or "evolutionary" work of language. I like that view; it gets preverbs excited; they start talking. I register language getting worked up, a certain intensity gathering in the stomach, a sense of energy rising in the cerebral-spinal column and spreading into the thinking hands / fingers ... more favorite configurations. I give myself permission to follow these sudden permissions. I gently restrain my inherited censors. I trust preverbial language to edit itself in process. Trust—an important value within the process—trust of lingual intelligence. The view: I don't *have* this intelligence; I'm *inside* intelligence. And this is a way of elucidating navigation in lingual psychonautics.

There's a "how to read" (to use Pound's formulation) implicit in any poetics. Preverbs alert the mind that the will to interpret may easily become a hunt for ideology, or an unacknowledged effort to reify an ontology beyond its occasion. The preverbial poem doesn't "put things into words" or fail to do that or embody the frustration of the unsayable; it lets words lead mind into "further things." I sometimes characterize this furthering as *the state of poetry*; that state has a kind of feeling tone that seems to come of its own accord, but thinking I know what that means does not produce more poetry. A preverb causes the mind to reflect on its own process, but it does not rest in reflection; there are other things for it to (not) do.

Fink: I want to explore the idea that you "do not construct" preverbs. You hesitate to use the verb "receive," but you do acknowledge that "they weave through" your "thinking... in response to other thinking/ reading...." Your receptivity to a host of other conversations and texts is acknowledged as an influence, but this is not the same as a transmission from a single source. You stress the preverb's emergence as a feeling "in the mind *and* in the body." Regarding the latter, you speak of "intensity gathering in the stomach, a sense of energy rising in the cerebral-spinal column and spreading into the thinking hands/fingers," and regarding the former, I wonder if it's internal audition or internal envisionment of the words or both. My other question is if all preverbs that manifest this mental and kinesthetic emergence are kept for inclusion in a poem or if you later make an editorial decision that a particular sentence does not pass muster and will not be included in a poem.

Quasha: Speaking generally about agency in poetry, what actually makes the poem, text-generation is probably best viewed as a sort of continuum, one end of which is deliberate construction, by whatever poetic principle, and the other end something like pure and spontaneous inspiration ("received"), whatever that in fact means. Probably most poetry is at best only approximately positioned somewhere along the continuum, even when it makes definite claims. Preverbs actively contemplate this poetic problem of source and agency, and so I can't take a firm position here without undermining the work's "uncertainty" principle. Yet there's always more to say, which is one reason why the agency issue implicitly or explicitly comes up inside the process of the poems.

I'm interested in the discourse of responding to impossible but necessary questions. My video project of the last thirteen years is relevant here—*art is/poetry is/music is (Speaking Portraits)*—in which I ask artists, poets and musicians to say what it (art/poetry/music) *is*: An impossible question to answer definitively, yet it's one that more or less continuously wants to be answered. We try, we fall short, we try again. The video project, which is very impersonal from my angle, relates to the poetics of preverbs as site of a discourse of indeterminate response. I've interviewed over a thousand artists/poets/musicians in eleven countries (amidst many languages), and my "art" there is in drawing people out to say what hasn't been said. I practice a certain receptiveness and open listening, focusing my mind on enabling them to make their most powerful statements about what "it" is, even as we allow that there isn't really an *it* as fixed object. There's an uncertainty principle at work: *Saying what art is changes what art is.* You ask me interesting difficult and ultimately impossible questions about the poetic process and that inspires new thoughts, and these in turn are reality-generating in my personal sense of what the poetic process is. You become co-creative with my sense of my "own" work—co-configurative within an emergent definitional awareness.

The preverbial interaction with this fact of actual interactivity of minds is to *reflect further*. I often play on Cocteau's film *Orphée* where the oracular radio says "The mirror would do well to reflect further." He draws out the double sense of reflection as both mirroring and self-reflection, as well as reflecting *on*. The dynamic of a preverb, which is always a line and a syntactic unit, contains a particular volatility in reflection, wherein verbal subject and verbal object are in play and interplay. We see ourselves in a mirror and reflect on what we see and, further, on the very fact that we are in a state of reflection, and so on. The preverb is generated out of this dynamic; it's an event of awareness inside language as its medium. As the poet I'm participating in a process of language action that is emergent as a happening within a charged inquiry-declaration.

I realize that this is a paradoxical construction (which may ultimately be the only kind of construction in the preverbial world). Inquiry-declaration/asking-saying. Provisional assertion/assertive provisionality. It's a liminality of distinctions. I experience language asking something of me, an embracing attention, a hands-on response to a demanding condition. Furthermore, I see a connection with the sculpture I've made, "axial stones" (documented and discussed in *Axial Stones: An Art of Precarious Balance*).[2] The stones come into radical precarious balance by my becoming the neutral space of listening to them; in a sense I *become* the interactive dynamic between the stones—I'm their momentary ligature. For this to happen I have to treat them with affection and let them guide me, we "converse" sometimes for hours on end. It has an eros, a connecting energy through attraction and response. (Eros, according to Plato, is a daimon, a between-entity connecting men and gods.)

I'm saying all this by way of indicating a modality of engaging the art medium, and I discovered it first in language (starting with Blake). The impulse to say something, speak from an emergent thought, starts the sentence, which in some way shows it has a sort of will of its own; one feels the pull and the rhythm, something like its breathing; its pulse. Instead of marshaling it toward a thought conclusion or conceptualized outcome, one listens in on its dynamic and allows minute adjustments to occur—further attractions to meaning. One discovers what is willing to be said. One is reading inside writing and writing the reading. Much like the speaking portraits (*art is/poetry is/music is*), the axial stones, and the axial drawing, the discipline of *listening in on* emergent language has a quite impersonal dimension, while of course it's intimately woven through one's personal concerns, experience, reading, thinking, etc. Is this a construction or a reception? Let's admit that these words are failing to account for the complexity of the event. (Complexity here has resonance with the mathematical sense of "chaos" or tracking dynamical systems, or a recent interest of mine, *self-organized criticality* as a model for poetics.) The concept terms we use do their work as far as they go, then comes the time to let go into something further. My sense of discipline is to accept the process and not interfere; an energy is moving forward yet in a state of radial release. A flexible copularity.

---

[2] *Axial Stones: An Art of Precarious Balance*, foreword by Carter Ratcliff (Berkeley: North Atlantic Books, 2006); hereinafter cited in text parenthetically.

You ask whether preverb-making involves "internal audition or internal envisionment of the words or both." Both and more. The whole body is a zone of mind activity. The gut has been called the second brain (see Michael Gershon's *The Second Brain*),[3] and some speak of the heart as a brain (resonating with Chinese and Sufi notions, for instance), and yet we typically think of poetics in cerebral terms alone. Charles Olson proposed *proprioception* (own-grasping) as a key to poetic thinking, a notion which he uses both metaphorically and literally. Physiologically proprioception stands for "unconscious perception of movement and spatial orientation arising from stimuli within the body itself." We move oriented by a complex interaction of factors (stimuli) internal (body) and external (physical space). In a line, a preverb, we get oriented, we get situated by engaging a sensory network and range. I *hear* a line *into* its action which becomes orientational on its own terms and *in* the terms themselves, as if walking through words, indeed *walking words*. They take their (our) steps in their (our) own preverbial space. Reading moves through these peripatetic events in a sort of mirroring action, engaging our mirror neurons (reading is doing)—and I see this too as a kind of proprioception. Language is itself proprioceptive inside us. The literal/metaphorical tangle gets woven in the text. The friction of engagement is also erotic.

You ask if I edit and reject lines once they are there. Of course; it's a process of constant (self)refinement. They mostly come whole yet sometimes emerge fragmentarily. For the first few years of preverbs—there were thousands already then—they were constantly coming and going; dropping in, dropping out; and over the years they often changed, but less and less in recent times. I learned how to feel "false flow"—that is, when the excitement of composition would keep on generating more, even when the grounded receptivity had waned. I realized that the preverbial process was teaching me something better than momentum.

[3] Michael Gershon, *The Second Brain: A Groundbreaking New Understanding of Nervous Disorders of the Stomach and Intestine* (New York: Harper Perennial, 1999).

Momentum is always getting ahead of itself, reaching for what it is not yet; overexcited. Axiality is about staying true to the center. It allows an inner release that clears out debris—a reflective clarity within the swirl of energic invention. There is willing retention, a certain holding back. One hears better. There are many subtle currents of meaning in process which one learns to register. It's a dynamic flow with discriminating awareness. Preverbial space allows for asking-declaring. I've thought of it as a possible mood of grammar—the performative indicative. Zero point composition: Each line gives up the momentum of the previous line and returns to zero.

Fink: In describing how the preverbs are read, you use the term "configuration," which I, perhaps wrongly, would just call "interpretation." Does configuration reflect the compounding of the original figuration of the preverb and the mind/body of the reader, the figure *together with* ("con") the reader's processing? Since you speak later in your response about the importance of context and level in reading preverbs, is configuration recontextualization or level-shifting of the figure? Or am I missing other resonances in the term configuration?

Quasha: A useful question to make a distinction. There is a big difference between *configuration* and *interpretation*, at least in my usage, although I suppose you could say interpretation is a developed or fixed form of configuration. Let's look at it practically: You pour cream into black coffee and look at it—what do you see? Passively: Enough, not enough, or too much cream. A little more awake to the moment: Wow, what a swirl! Very engaged in seeing: Look, a dragon! That's a range of intensity and concentration in viewing what's at hand. A matter of degree that verges on a difference of kind. There are different species of configuration based on modality of engagement. Some might call seeing "the dragon" an interpretation, but it's quicker than that, very immediate and very brief, changing instantly. Interpretation persists even while seeing the dragon disappear, causing the seeing to stop; alternatively you could ride the process and see further emergence. The dragon-seeing could map onto certain Taoist practices celebrated in ancient Chinese pottery, for instance. This extension of the seeing into an art- or religion-contextualized apperceptive thinking moves in the direction of interpretation; it takes the mind into a thinking process but it also stops the immediacy of perception-experiencing and further configuration. There are of course many micro-stages between these event extremes, and there is *a possible oscillatory engagement* that is its own kind of contemplation—feeling-thinking, thinking-sensing, etc. In normal consciousness we're *after* something and may see something before it's really there (I pour the cream and want to drink my coffee now; the swirl of black and white is little more than a charming delay).

What if we approach this consciously? For instance, I have learned to work certain minute practices within ordinary experience which create the extraordinary experience of what I call *conscious liminality*; the latter allows for an oscillatory intensity/release process that furthers configuration. This gazing level of experience can jump from viewing over into drawing or into language, for instance, wherein it finds a "further nature." If I'm preoccupied, it won't happen; I drink my coffee and move on. If I "space into" the experience, something very special might arise. In this frame of viewing—cream in coffee configuring—I might see nothing, no figuration, just movement. In bigger frames of experience and depending on my mind-set, or more seriously the health state of my organism, there might be a moment of (metaphorically) "apperceptive agnosia" or "failure" of perception; of course if that happens all the time it may be a symptom of cognitive disorder, but I'm focusing on *the fine line between expected order and allowable disorder*.

The brain seems to be hardwired to recognize and interpret anything experienced (part of our evolutionary survival orientation); this keeps us within the limits of biological normality. Blake protested staying within nature's "same dull round over again" because he saw the visionary potential of the "Human Imagination Divine" as going beyond—consciously evolving out of— current human limitations, which among other things sustain human violence and social-political "tyranny" (his word, but more and more our reality). Every act of perception is either a repetitive trap or an opportunity for standing outside past/pattern/limitation (a meaning of "ecstasy" is "standing beside"). This is a long way of saying that the *configurative*, in my usage, is different from interpretative in allowing a self-generating process of *axiality* (on-center experiencing) and *conscious liminality* (the open oscillatory between-experiencing). Together they comprise a single complex principle: Axial-Liminal-Configurative.

You ask if configuration means "the figure *together with* ('con') the reader's processing," and the short answer is yes. Preverbial reading foregrounds reader option. Reading enters a path (a line) and a rhythmic event with multiple options. The lines are, relative to perhaps more familiar poetic lines, quite open to variable emphasis, leading to different meaning-options within an existing range determined by specific semantics, grammar, and suprasegmental phonemic options in saying the line (e.g., light housekeeping vs. lighthouse keeping). All of these lingual vectors are highly variable for the most part throughout preverbs. The lingual array is not arbitrary or manipulative but arises within an evolved preverbial process which axial poetics has taught me over the years to be responsive to. The poem is in waiting for a reader's engagement to take it on a meaning-journey through variably significant territory. There is no final or right interpretation for a preverb, but any interpretation is potentially attractive.

Preverbs are disciples of Blake's phrase: "Every thing possible to be believ'd is an image of truth."

Fink: We have already discussed your questioning of authorial authority, but we have not explicitly foregrounded the representation of the self in your preverbs. Since, for Blake, and for you, perception is most valuable as a way of breaking through limitation rather than reinforcing it, one form of exploration that I configure in your books of preverbs is the configuring of possible multiplication of selves, as opposed to the constitution of a unitary self. I could cite many examples, especially from *Things Done for Themselves*, but I'll confine myself to a handful. "Song of itself" (*pace* Whitman) begins with the contrary motions of the emotional awareness of the displacement of an authoritative self or, in Joseph Lease's term "representative I," and a command to a guest to bar access to other guests, other selves: "I showed up feeling I was not the one expected to be seen. / *Welcome to my poem. Lock the door*" (*Things Done for Themselves*, 37). Later in the poem, there is both expectation of otherness within the self *and* the paradoxical sense that the comforts of home must somehow stem from this otherness: "I'm expecting. The surface is feeling itself. / You'd have to want to be someone else to feel at home." Language itself occasions awareness of the split(ting) self, like the splitting of the speaker and the spoken, but instead of mourning the loss of unity, instead of being nostalgic, "speech is only natural in the roots" makes this multiplication an occasion for linguistic play:

> Sometimes my language tells me who's speaking and sometimes not.
> Like now.
>
> And then. The *I* I count on asks why so secret....
>
> Grammar is getting from here to there strictly between us.
>
> Identity under open pressure has a mounting weirdness quotient....
>
> Seeing I'm here hears the contrary.
>
> My thought dangling modifies from behind.
>
> (*Glossodelia Attract,* 32)

The "mounting weirdness quotient"—for example, in the homonymic synesthesia and grammatical doubling or tripling of the penultimate line above—not only puts simple notions of "identity" "under... pressure" but *opens* identity to betweenness ("between us"). If "my biography invents me in its own image" ("a likely tall tale," *Daimon of the Moment*, 44), then that "image" is like a dangling modifier of "thought" that does not quite accurately join the representation and its object, especially because its object is a process, and any "biography" is a temporary measure.

As you think about poems in these books of preverbs that manifest a preoccupation with shifting notions of identity, how do you account for the persistence of this dynamic? In your configurations, do you align the thinking/feeling of selfhood with other thematic topoi, such as space/ time, body/mind, absence/presence, substantiality/insubstantiality? And are you thinking through and perhaps departing from the findings of poetic, philosophical, or other precursors?

Quasha: I'm enjoying your reading of preverbs, and the strange part of the experience is that it takes me in and out of recognizing "my" text, rather refreshing like seeing someone new in the mirror. There's a curious sense of alienation—something like a *Verfremdungseffekt* in the Brechtian sense, a distancing or alienation—"playing in such a way that the audience was hindered from simply identifying itself with the characters in the play," he famously wrote about Chinese acting and what he sought in theater. And this shows me that your reading of texts which I present under my name is something like a performance I attend and cannot fully identify with the players (the lines, the readings)—there's pushback. Your poignant reading is something new for me. I cherish this experience as a kind of demonstration of the principle of the poem: It resists a reader's (in this case *my*) effort to identify with what is being read, to use it personally rather than to stand beyond personal confines. If there's a mimesis in the poetic process it's of something not on the page (the stage) but of an only-now-occurring activity between performance and reception. And unexpectedly this effect points to the way I can address your question about self.

Self is a word-concept for a fundamental but controversial "reality." It is of such complexity that a vast array of philosophical, psychological, social, and religious views could be invoked, and if the preverb process continues long enough, many of those views may strut their stuff on this stage. I may well have believed in many of them for some span of time from moments to years, but now I have preverbs to prevent my attachment to any one of them for more than, perhaps, a line. Yet they can still show up as things "possible to be believed." So a discourse issue here is to what extent I can discuss identity without lapsing into self-generating language which quickly tends toward the preverbial. (Of course an interview, like anything thought or said in life, will have its naturally axial moments that stay in motion even as we grasp them.) Concepts here are placeholders for engaged attention; they're not restful removals from the field of action. I study self, but more from within the moment of awareness grounded in present experience than theoretically. I could mark this a discourse of *self[-]study unfolding in language.*

You ask about "the representation of the self" but of course I should emphasize (what you already know) that it is not quite accurate to say that preverbs *represent.* Or what seems like representation is at best a phase in emergent linguality (reality-generating language). Self is a word-concept that is doing something for the speaker/thinker. The metaphor of an actor on the stage comes to mind again because I have the sense of watching what is happening from some distance. There is a poetic dimension of self that opens up in the process of self-reflection; the poem *gives sign* that it knows what it's doing. At times it seems the poem itself has *self.* It occupies a range between sentience and sapience. Poetic process, as I know it, is not only self-reflective, it's reflexive. *Song of itself.*

To set a sort of meta-context, I point to the sheer complexity of the word *self* in its play throughout language, the way language plays out the possibilities of identity. The *word*-self, the self constituted in word use, performs any social interaction with qualities of the moment, both personal and contextual. Think of Charlie Chan's innovative subject pronoun *Humble self* and its variants— "*Humble countenance merely facing facts.*" (Taken out of context this one has preverbial potential!) On another level it's like the problematic of mind seeing itself, or as Alan Watts colorfully observed: "Trying to define yourself is like trying to bite your own teeth." And of course one way or another we the people do this all the time. But we may not be catching our own act. That's a job for poetry.

Your question above, citing lines from three books, illuminates itself quite successfully, pointing to the non-expectation of unity of self and instead occasioning multiplicity and the embrace of inevitable otherness in the site of "identity." Aberrations in grammar (like "dangling modifier") play out possibilities of object relations, given the confusions of subject and object. I see these irregularities as *diversity*, including something like the vital importance of biodiversity as against the life-weakening effects of its loss to monoculture. Prescriptive grammar is functionally a force of anti-diversity and weakens language in part by destabilizing speakers, who are culturally impeded from discovering self-authorization and self-regulation in language. Poetry in this sense, as intrinsically unauthorized, models open reality possibility. Multiplicity of self gives evidence of multiversality (an often more useful idea than universality). Any kind of pre-established authority in language obscures its eco-sensitivity. The destruction of ecosystems begins in flawed and insensitive descriptions of reality, reductive attitudes toward our interactive situatedness on this planet, and indeed in life. We lose our intrinsic ability to engage with diverse living realities, and they in turn lose their voice. We silence "nature" in presuming its silence. *We make things dumb dumbing things down.* (Later preverb)

Multiple selves have multiple idioms. Accordingly I declare a mission in poetry, at least implicitly, to explore language in its widest possibility, which might mean interspecifically. Self itself has interspecies connectivity. Anyone who has lived with animals in any degree of intimacy knows they speak; the linguality in common may involve even more communing than communicating. Poetic space gains unnamed sensitivities from this kind of extra-species resonance. From any perspective other than intimate this level of experience has a high WQ (weirdness quotient).

This level of poetic focus once implied a Romantic lineage, although there are plausible roots as well in the Renaissance (Pico della Mirandola, Giordano Bruno); but now of course it's supported by so-called hard science, in particular ethology with its almost daily revelations of pervasive communication in nature. This is not the place to argue interspecies intelligence, which has interested me since my 20s when I encountered Roger Payne's work on humpback whale songs and John Lilly's *The Mind of the Dolphin*; in my poetry journal of that time, *Stony Brook*, which launched *ethnopoetics* with Jerome Rothenberg, I tried to find someone to explore a comparable poetic discipline with biopoetic force (I imagined an "ecopoetics," now of course happening, and more), but apparently it was too early or I didn't have the right connections. It's worth noting the popular titles that register the recent shift in biological perspective: Jeremy Narby's *Intelligence in Nature*; Michael Pollan's *The Botany of Desire* and "The Intelligent Plant" (*New Yorker,* December 2013); Daniel Chamovitz's *What a Plant Knows*; and the 2013 PBS film *What Plants Talk About.* Ethnopoetics of course registered preliterate poetries sympathetic to interspecies dynamics, but discovering the implications for a more-than-human or a posthumanist perspective requires a subtler inquiry into how our own language *already* works. In other words, it's not the strange and unfamiliar phenomena that I find most compelling here, but what we do and say that manifests a more complex axiality that redefines us. Our syntax springs leaks that open larger cracks, even windows, onto our broad interconnectedness. Preverbial poetics maintains a certain vigilance for these events of showing through. Self is permeable.

The notions of self and identity come into play throughout preverbs, and each shift in perspective resonates across the others. I sometimes theorize a *logoic butterfly effect*: Every word action in preverbs may affect reading actions throughout the poems, in fact between books. Every word event reconditions the field of word events pervasively. (Perhaps one could think of this as *noespheric resonance.*) It's like pulling one thread in a fabric—the whole fabric pulls into it. We "think body" this way in (hands-on) bodywork (which I have practiced for a few decades and is a source of "axial thinking"): Doing anything to any part of the body impacts the whole. Like the body the poem is organismic on many levels. (I mean this quite a bit more radically than older notions like "organic form," but also not as a limit of formal concepts; it's difficult to imagine a limit to the ways of conceptualizing form.) We impart *self* to language: Whatever is true of ourselves becomes in some way true in our language-making. Whatever self is, it's part of the field and it acts by field. In a sense this is fractal-like in that *self nature* is scale-invariant. It shows up locally and impacts globally.

What I just called axial thinking registers in language for me as preverbs. They happen at times in response to other thinking—you ask if they're "thinking through and perhaps departing from the findings of poetic, philosophical, or other precursors"—yes but serendipitously, book in hand, overhearing a conversation at a neighboring table (kledomanticly), gathering "from the air a live tradition" (Pound, "Canto LXXXI"), as opposed to a systematic engagement with someone's thought or writing. The practice has a contemplative side, a kind of psychonautics, a centripetal quality of going in and out of balance along an edge, and a sort of slack-rope syntactics while crossing a micro-abyss.

Certain phrases we read stay with us for many years and evolve along a new track, perhaps becoming something that would be unrecognizable to the originator. An example for me would be Stevens' "The poem of the mind in the act of finding / What will suffice...." In my case the notion of "suffice" is indeterminate.

Fink: From the tenuousness and provisional aspect of any configuration of the self, let's move to the topic of love, of communion with an other, which is a significant component of all four preverb books, especially, I think, *Verbal Paradise* and *Things Done for Themselves*. This time, I'll confine myself to one brief example. Here is part of the opening section of "Bottling Up":

> She swings in her body tall with these trees.
>
> Almost known is almost to have been....
>
> Words audition.
>
> *Is that you calling?* I must be overhearing.
>
> Almost knowing, almost being, almost telling.
>
> Flow.
>
> So she shows. *(Verbal Paradise,* 31*)*.

Once more, I'm gonna configure for a minute. The "flow" of the erotic frisson in the opening line gives way to epistemological uncertainty. If we cannot know our selves enduringly, if "finding / what will suffice" of self-knowledge is a process that never reaches total fulfillment, the other, at best, is "almost known." Presumption of total knowledge of the other, total communication with her, and insufficient attention to her and to the relationship as "flow" that "she shows" (as does the lover) are the path to idealization that will breed a deadly, reifying, if tempting immortality, as in a fair amount of love poems and songs in the last few millennia: "*Poetry resists immortality with difficulty.* Like love" (32). Well, Stevens understood the problem of immortality when he titled a section of *Notes Toward a Supreme Fiction* "It Must Change." Poetry must change to stay alive; love must change. "Words" always "audition," because the words can't be assured of getting the part—that is, the attainment of full communication, whatever that would be. The lover here is not presenting a rhetorical question when he apostrophizes the beloved to ask if she is "calling" or calling him. It's an actual question. She might be addressing herself or someone else, and he is merely "overhearing" what is not meant for him, even if she seems to be speaking to him. In no way am I saying that this poem is promulgating a pessimistic view of love and communication but that possibilities of success and failure are built into any structure of utterance ("telling"). Indeed, "No line's too long that lengthens in longing" (33); reaching passionately for the other is "how I know I'm here, and with..." (32).

There is no simple answer to Tina Turner's question, "What's love got to do with it?"—when "it" is your preverbial poetry, or just about anything else. So I'm eager to hear your answer(s) to this impossible question.

Quasha: I'm going to begin responding to this, as you say, "impossible question" in a kind of basic way, because it takes us to the heart of my poetic orientation—with, however, advance apologies to Tina for inadequately answering her question.

"Epistemological uncertainty" is only one kind of uncertainty, which foregrounds our (in)ability to "justify" belief or other levels of assessment. Of course it's pervasive throughout preverbs, but there are other kinds of uncertainty as well—psychological, especially emotional;

indeed *ontological*; amongst others. In a general historical perspective Heisenberg's uncertainty principle has destabilizing impact, which may be viewed as inevitable; that's what uncertainty does at any level and in virtually any context. But it's not a negative factor, unless we experience it so; intrinsically it's neither positive nor negative. It's the condition of what can or cannot be known, which might be circumstantial. What is difficult for the mind is to embrace uncertainty and allow the *uncertainty state*, as it were, to teach us; to open us to unfamiliar knowing. Uncertainty can be *initiatic* in that it introduces us to new kinds of awareness which certainty, for all its service to mental stability, occludes. Openness in this sense involves non-resistance, a certain release of grip, and a willingness to at least temporarily *not know*. And not judge. The attitude here is as relevant to the scientist as the meditator. I wish to track its relevance to poetic process and reading.[4]

There are unspecified kinds of uncertainty, unnamed ones that don't fit our available categories. One that I work with could be called *readerly uncertainty*. This shows up simply, for instance, as *what is this I'm reading?* We take a stand on meaning, or at least the operative question, if we do continue on, or else we might give up prematurely. If we have a lot of experience reading a certain type of text we may assume that the meanings make sense in accordance with precedent. But that might not work out. Preverbs work with *not working out*. They embody destabilized meanings and narratives that lead to meaning. My preoccupation with *uncertainty process* is related to what I said earlier: I'm interested in the discourse of responding to impossible but necessary questions. Preverbs declare a certain productive uncertainty in discourse.

This is a warm-up to responding to your highly specified concern that names *love*, and in a sense I could say again everything I said about *self*. It's a word-concept for a fundamental but controversial "reality." And the two go together. We tend to understand loving as something the self

---

[4] Quasha has theorized "Uncertainty" more extensively in a paper of that name on Robert Kelly's "poetics of singularity" in *Talisman: A Journal of Contemporary Poetry and Poetics*, #44 (2016): http://www.talismanmag.net; also online at academia.edu.

does. And of course historically we discriminate different kinds of love, such as the four-love ancient Greek system: simplistically speaking, *agape* ("unconditional love"), *phileo* ("platonic love"), *storge* ("familial love"), and *eros* ("romantic/passionate love," including sexual). And there are other systems, such as the biblical three (minus *storge*) where *agape* takes on the divine-love register. And then there are the Eastern refinements and extensions known as Tantric and Taoist love which are meditative and transformational and bear some relation to Western Alchemy, Hermeticism, etc. I mention this complexity to indicate the prima facie difficulty of simply speaking about love. Preverbs are deeply tuned in to this complexity and often work multiple levels as options of reading a given line, not referentially so much as structurally (syntactic, semantic, etc.).

Which brings me to the "how to read" concern in readerly uncertainty. The Poundian how-to-read presumed a high-culture standard based on preferred historical models, an approach that was in different ways challenged by his contemporaries: for instance, Gertrude Stein, who created unprecedented language processes that caused a suspension, willing or not, of belief *or* disbelief. The initial impact of her work, like that of *Finnegans Wake* or Dada texts, was particular kinds of readerly disruption. So readerly uncertainty is nothing new. But the function of uncertainty varies significantly with different discourse approaches.

I'm interested in the *optionality of meaning*, in part as a way beyond our mostly private fundamentalisms. Take the example you chose. Because the poem images a female person at the beginning (*She swings in her body tall with these trees*) you seem to assume her presence throughout; this is one option. But preverbs are line-intensive and do not promise continuity or narrativity, although these also are configurative options. So the line opening the next quoted stanza—*Words audition*—is held within a progression that has "the lover" apostrophizing "the beloved" and asking "if she is 'calling' or calling him," which you take to be "an actual question," and so on. I can see how a way of reading poetry supports this, and the narrative allows you to consider that the poem is not "promulgating a pessimistic view of love and communication" but allowing "that possibilities of success and failure are built into any structure of utterance ('telling')." I do not approach the poem this way but I do indeed entertain the same conclusion about any structure of utterance. There may be multiple paths to an insight.

It's hard to explain this precisely but I want to say that the sequence of lines isn't constructed so that it "promulgates" something; rather, it allows constructive reading as an option. *Words audition* is quite interestingly glossed by your "words can't be assured of getting the part," which I like a lot (almost a preverb itself). That takes the word "audition," so to speak, at its word. (I do experience words as auditioning during the composition, because often multiple words try to get in.) But there is another way that words come to mean in preverbs, as I suggested earlier with "logoic butterfly effect," which is by *processual context-pressure.* "Audition" appears a number of times throughout preverbs in ways that draw out the etymology as "listening." This is an example of how multiple readings over time produce different word resonance—(to attract readers willing to read this way could be any poet's dream). The fact that preverbs have evolved over a seventeen year period (and inherited many years of axial poems before that, including the long work *Somapoetics* from the early '70s), indicates a basis of this kind of reading. *Lines signify radially* is the principle of meaning-by-field. It points to *multiple reading dimensions,* not layered as coded or referential meaning or allegory, but an actual *text dimensionality,* embodied in language structure.

Returning to the passage you cited (the line following "Words audition"): "*Is that you calling?* I must be overhearing," which you read as a personal question as to whether the beloved is calling—a reasonable assumption within the dimension of the personal. There are other, non-personal dimensions operative here in the "bottling up" of meaning (about love, amongst other things), inquiring as to the status of the text itself, its source, the overlay on or of the personal, the question of (a) "calling" (another strongly field-resonant word), and the implication that poetic reception is a kind of overhearing (kledomanticly again)—whether of the beloved or of something not so easily configured.

Is "calling" the "same" when recurring? Gertrude Stein's repetitive words, phrases and syntactic patterns lead to a discovery that there is no actual repetition, but rather a moving through language that is the opportunity for further insight along a language path of *emergent* awareness. Language is the medium of *telling*; poetics is the evolving guide to help us allow that to happen, unobstructed. The discipline is a gradual tuning in and discovery of a non-controlling-control or principle of self-regulation wherein we learn to let the saying occur as it will. It's in part a discipline of getting out of our own way. We follow a feeling tone inside a language tone, which depending on the poetic modality may be an *actual word sound toning* (like Robert Duncan's use of Pound's "tone-leading of vowels"), a *semantic toning*, and/or something like *syntactic toning*. How much these ideas communicate depends on the particular experience of the reader.

The goal of the poem is to engage the mind so that the poetic principle takes hold and makes a specific kind of reading possible. Depending on the evolving poetics, one hopes the singularity of reading, once made possible, may in the end be powerful for those who get with it. The uncertainty process is characterized by a logoic *jouissance* chastened by disrupted certainty in our cherished interpretations. My experience is that it contributes to alteration of readerly consciousness.

Identity/self/love.... A later preverb says: *I have to learn the faces of face-offs the heart generates.* Instead of a problematic Freudian slip, I follow a language self that "aimlessly" utters self-conflicting emergent sayings while courting life complexity. There is "self" projection the "*I*" doesn't recognize, which to "know myself" I have to get to know. Words are masks, ranging between the Greek theater persona to the modern disguise (I grew up on the Lone Ranger; Antigone came later) and on to what in preverbs gets called the *impersona.*

This is admittedly a somewhat difficult art to get oriented to. My memory is that I first discovered this kind of reading in my mid-20s in studying Blake (but it may have actually begun with my intense joy in discovering T.S. Eliot, especially *Four Quartets*, at age 14 while understanding little and not really caring). Poetics in this sense is a species of mindfulness in poetry, the mind tracking its own surrenders, such that neither meta-awareness nor passionate engagement fully dissolves. In the present stage of poetic history this kind of internal dialogue between a poetry and its poetics is not unusual, and it could be viewed as one outcome of T.S. Eliot's post-Metaphysical emphasis on overcoming the "dissociation of sensibilities." One question is how well the mutually corrective balance is kept throughout, and that is difficult to answer, since any new equilibrium of poetic energy and aesthetic judgment is slow in developing in the wake of a truly alive new poetic force. (I hold that it is not the poet's business to worry one's place in history or relative "merit" or who's on first; I agree with Duchamp that judgment belongs to the future.)

I rarely recall what motivated particular preverbs. They are not motivated by my having something to say in the ordinary sense. On a personal level, awareness that includes love is central to my life, but it's not consistently clear how that relates to preverbs, since they're not selling attitudes. I dedicate every book to Susan Quasha (I see her as preverbs' truest reader, along with Charles Stein, from the beginning) but it is not an indication that the *she/her* of the text either is or is not her person. It could be an *aspect* of her mind or perhaps someone else or no *one*; it could be *my* mind since preverbs sometimes appear to identify poetic process as female gender—the "poet"—and one series is called *Fluctuant Gender.* I'm not opposed to seeing the poetic process as in some sense love-sustaining, even eros-centered, and I confess to enjoying, say, Ibn Arabi on "intelligence of the heart." But knowing any of this should not predispose reading to any particular conclusion. *A truth knows its name thanks to its contrary,* says a preverb down the road.

Fink: I'd like to conclude my part of this dialogue by soliciting an important aspect of your sense of the book as book (its "bookness") or perhaps, instead, as "book" under erasure. Although my last two questions were informed by somewhat conventional thematic rubrics, they were merely meant as a point of departure: I did realize (and "certainly" should understand by now!) that multiple contexts engender numerous possibilities of interpretation and defamiliarization for an individual preverb, and the complexity multiplies further when one configures a poem, even more when one configures a book of preverbs. This being said, and acknowledging that you have spoken of an intuitive process of composition, characterized by trial and error, I note that *Glossodelia Attract* and *Things Done for Themselves,* which you characterize as two books in one, both appeared in 2015 and *The Daimon of the Moment* is making its appearance this year (2016), so I can surmise that the chronology of composition does not dictate the architecture of these (separate) books. I wonder whether you as author reached a realization, after the fact or *in medias res*, that there has been a rationale—whether visual or auditory or kinesthetic or multisensory, and undoubtedly rhizomatic—for your decision to gather particular preverb poems into one of these books and others into a second and still others into the third. And if this is the case, can you give us a sense of the contours of that rationale or cluster of perceived patterns, as it might be useful for readers to include a version of your architectural intentionality in the process of their configuring?

Quasha: Again let's go from simplest to more complex. I have a quite precise and unmysterious definition of *book* with respect to preverbs: "A book here is defined as seven 'preverb-complexes' or poem-series of varying length."[5] That structural decision is arbitrary, meaning that it is not symbolic or meaningful but purely practical in that it makes for a convenient and approximate book length overall; and it applies to all ten books to date. A conceptual aspect of preverbs is non-symbolic form; rather, form as fixed container like a wine glass, and it applies to all levels. The first unit is *the line* (no run-overs) delimited by the word-processing default line (MS Word); the next unit is *the page*, which in a poem-series is a single poem numbered and titled; then *the series*, which is the one open distinction—anything from several pages to over thirty, so far. A *book* is seven poem-series, plus a preface and sometimes a poetics statement at the end (at the beginning uniquely in *Verbal Paradise*). One rationale for these arbitrary units is that it's rather like life: We fit into neutral given structures (60-minute hour, 7-day week, 4-wheel cars, a

[5] Footnote in "Pre Gloss," *Glossodelia Attract (preverbs)*, xii.

given body size, a limited lifespan, etc.) and for the most part we make do, since these containers allow for an infinite variety of content and quality of experience. It's a choice, to see it, say, as an enclosed garden (*hortus conclusus*) or to bang against the prison bars.

Beyond that I have a rather minimalist sense of overall design, which allows me to concentrate on intensive language events without dressing them up externally. A seeming exception is that the books have strong visual covers, all using my axial drawings/paintings (Dakini Series) and designed by Susan Quasha. So far all of the publishers have allowed us to follow this approach (Zasterle Press, Marsh Hawk Press, Talisman House Press, and our own Station Hill of Barrytown). But the decision to use what at first glance seems like similar cover art has the heuristic value that people having trouble telling one book from another must pay real attention; then they see the real difference. Same with the interior: Lines ask to be known individually, not because they fit a pattern or are part of a development, narrative, or formal symbolism, but according to the intrinsic event of the line, which is highly variable in rhythm, content, syntax, diction, etc. Everything must speak for itself, without supervening justification. Every line, poem, series, and book asks the reader to be willing to return to zero. No predictable momentum. No overall abstraction as regards style or meaning. No cultural validation by precedent. Everything follows a core minimally definable principle. One of several names I use for the principle is *zero point poetics*, another is *axiality*.

There is minimal "architectural intentionality," to use your term. The architecture, like, say, a geodesic dome, is a structural principle that allows for maximum variability of operative intentionality within a simply defined container. In a sense the principle is scale invariant (short series, long series; short book [*Verbal Paradise*], long book [*Glossodelia Attract*]). And, contrary to your impression, the books are in fact basically chronological within the book but not necessarily from book to book.[6] That is, the poems/series in each book were created in the same

---

[6] The order of the books is mainly circumstantial. In 2010 Manuel Brito of Zasterle Press in the Canary Islands asked for a shorter book which corresponded

time span (say, six months to a year+), and when there are seven series it's a book. The numbered poems within each of the seven series in a book are written in order (though the lines within them may or may not be), but in the final order of the book the series may or may not stay in the order of creation—for no good reason beyond liking it that way. On the whole a book contains poems in series from a single sweep of time; it has a sort of overall atmosphere, which however does not translate into consistency, stylistic or otherwise. So there's no decision necessary about what goes in a given book. Choices are not self-consciously aesthetic or significantly conceptual. They do not "labor to be beautiful" (Yeats); they labor, as in birthing, to allow beauty, potentially "terrible," to be itself without the intervention of taste.

This was not all clear from the beginning seventeen years ago, when preverbs started out as an accumulation of individually generated lines with no concept of discrete parts beyond collected bunches of lines with titles (a "poem" was over a hundred lines single-spaced and no breaks). That was true for about the first 5,000 lines (some of which did get published online in the first couple of years, which I regretted). It evolved, like everything in preverbs, by something like *self-organized criticality* (SOC). That rather specialized physics term was introduced to me a few years ago by the Scottish nano-physicist James Gimzewski (UCLA),

---

to the length of the earlier preverb series and books; so the first published book, *Verbal Paradise* (2011), is also the earliest written. Burt Kimmelman made the next connection, with Marsh Hawk Press, and I decided to combine two early shorter books (the 4th and 5th written), *Things Done for Themselves* and *Witnessing the Place Awake*, naming it after the former, and temporarily skipping over the two short intervening books (2nd and 3rd written), still unpublished (*Black Scintillation* and *Eyes Take Away What They See*). Ed Foster then accepted *The Daimon of the Moment* for Talisman House Press, the 7th written, which is the first of the longer books that are now the norm (the intervening 6th, a shorter book, *Listening on a Curve*, still unpublished). *Glossodelia Attract* (the 8th book of preverbs) is the next in line chronologically, which I wanted for Station Hill for personal reasons. There are two subsequent unpublished books, the 9th and 10th (*White Holes* and *Alternate Lingualities* [changed to *Not Even Rabbits Go Down This Hole* (2020)]). Five longer series from the later books are published as chapbooks in print or online as of February 2016.

working with the artist Victoria Vesna, and it helped me understand how preverbs had evolved from the level of single line to poem to book. Frankly there were important gaps in my retrospective understanding of the uncertainty process which became somewhat clearer when I thought about it using the concept of SOC. Defined technically as "a property of (classes of) dynamical systems that have a critical point as an attractor," it describes an approach to complexity in which a system with many units interacting locally has an unpredictable critical threshold for change globally. Studying the part will not predict the behavior of the whole. Examples include the weather, earthquakes, the global economy, and, recently, brain activity—now poetry. The base is the old but continuously refined idea of *self-organization*, describing overall order emerging out of local interactions, the smaller components of an initially disordered system, or chaos.

I was inspired by Blake's "Proverbs of Hell" in *The Marriage of Heaven and Hell* to trust the space of the line to allow unlimited dynamics, including the transgressive. Persistent progression as accumulation over years began to reveal operative principles which became increasingly self-defining. The important thing was to stay with the process, daily if possible, as a practice, even when it's mystifying or even perplexing—an attitude rather like Keats' "negative capability" (or later for me "positive non-capability"). Quite suddenly a threshold would show up and preverbs crossed over into a new level of organization: Instead of three pages of single-spaced lines, groups formed, eventually stanza-like units of two or more lines. Meanwhile lines would fall away and new ones would replace them. Then the next level of sudden organization became the contained page, which after a while took on numbers and, later, titles, followed by series, then books. The process became *intelligent* in its own right, and ordering became articulate in relation to my level of sustained trust in the self-organizing process. It would feel like walking in dense woods and coming to a clearing. Poetic process became a primary teacher, and it interacted with like experience in drawing/painting and music, as well as video. I discovered that art practices based on *principle* rather than cultural precedent or concept can be intimately co-performative.

From the beginning preverbs have come mostly preformed and performative in the ear-mind. I write them in a notebook I carry with me everywhere, ever ready to write because I have about thirty seconds before they recede into the noesphere, back to the wild (perhaps to be picked up on by some other poet). The principle by which lines were and are selected for inclusion in a given poem underway, or for that matter are edited out or reformed during inclusion, I regard as *dowsing*—the pen as doodlebug or divining rod, so to speak, an indicative conduit. You could call it *syntax witching*. I gravitate toward this sort of metaphor of the unexplainable because the process is self-generating, not contrived or rationally focused or adapted for aesthetic effect. It's a nodal event that comes with a body-sense aura, which over time one gets better at distinguishing from mental babble. A sharp incursion of the unknown attractor.

George Quasha balancing Axial Stones #33

Vyt Bakaitis

Postscript

A Few Words for George Quasha and *poetry is (Speaking Portraits)*[1]

For more than half a century now, George Quasha has been an original, pedigreed multi-tasker as poet, musician, visual artist, mind-bending anthologist, and hands-on physical tai ch'i tactician—in short, a magus to unlock and lift a guiding presence out of the passing moment.

When I think of the work that Quasha is doing, balancing comes to mind, again and again, and in abundance: the kind of balance I can find, without stressing too hard, or reaching too far, in the name itself, at a glance, face value, syllabically and numerically in balance. The first name is singular, George, but the two strokes combined in Quasha immediately suggest, by an added beat, three. George Qua-sha. The sequence is simple in its progression, and familiar in the ordinary way that a thought will stir itself to a pronouncement, a micro-model in countering, buttressing dialogue. Even if kept to oneself, or playfully reversed, Magyar style, into Quasha George, the triangulation swiftly evokes the *voilà* of an ongoing dialectic.

---

[1] This note was first prepared for the presentation of *poetry is (Speaking Portraits)*, Vol. II, at Anthology Film Archives, New York City, on June 6, 2015. The full program for the event, co-organized by Kimberly Lyons and the present writer, included screenings and panels with poets, but due to time-constraints this introduction was not delivered on that occasion. The full-to-date combined project *art is/music is/poetry is (Speaking Portraits)* is now available for viewing online at www.art-is-international.org. *poetry is*—like its companions *art is* and *music is*—asks practitioners to say what it (poetry, art, music) is. Quasha has filmed over a thousand practitioners in eleven countries since 2002, and the project is ongoing; in 2006 he received a Guggenheim Foundation Fellowship in video art in part for this project.

To be adept in managing each instance into such balance wills the spine and skeleton under the full weight of a living person to get to stay in balance and advance, though hobbled by the necessity, step by step over the preordained course of three common human stages young Oedipus once guessed at.

Key watchwords are interlinked: *axial / liminal / configurative.*

All form the kind of balance that aligns rather than limits, that allows for movement but does not restrict it, is not pivotal but axial, and stays expansive in the way we may accept each definition as one of the reference lines within a flexible, immutably coordinated system. But no, forget *system*; make that *network*. And the evidence tells us, in this occasion of essays on George Quasha's achievement, it is a live network of responsive contributions: clear-eyed, wide-eyed, spanning.

Quasha works in language as well as in body-language, and he has worked the latter into a texture that announces itself as variously in words as in music, and without words or sounds into an expanding portfolio of sure-handed drawings. Moreover, the prolific, stacked instances of his chosen axial stones show their basic weight and brunt raised from time-worn primordial anonymity, since all stone in its settled natural state, no matter the scale, whether volcanic or sea-scoured, survives as detritus of dead inorganic matter. So his axial handling hints at an upsurge that, with each shaping guiding compassionate touch, comes to signal a coherent, consummate wholeness. In each attempt, the spell is immediate, a supple, improvised performance, with stunning energy uncoiled into a balance.

As an essential poetry, Quasha's books speak beyond volume: *Amanita's Hymnal / Magic Spell for the Far Journey*, 1971-72; *Somapoetics*, 1973; *Word-Yum*, 1974; *Giving the Lily Back Her Hands*, 1979; *Ainu Dreams*, 1999. And lately the open-ended exploratory series of "preverbs," starting with *Verbal Paradise*, 2011, has each of the seven volumes (as of 2021) rise to axiomatic gravitas from a commonplace field of riddling paroxysms. He also collaborated on putting together two substantial anthologies, that to this day remain monumental: *Open Poetry* (with Ronald Gross et al.) and *America a Prophecy* (with Jerome Rothenberg); both appeared in 1973. In the first he made the case for a metapoetry, in principles that apply in his work to this day; in the second he allied himself into a marvelously venturesome bond of community with fellow poets that continues to hold. In 1974, almost as if to attest a staying power to poetry's timely, intimate agency, George co-edited *An Active Anthology* with Susan Quasha, the artist/photographer who was then and still remains his wife. *Ainu Dreams*, first published in 1999, grew out of a collaboration on original dream poems with artist Chie Hasegawa (now Hammons).

Balance may be brought to any point at which you find yourself. Even while standing stock still you stay alert to the possibility of movement, if only to see ahead how you will fit in with what you see around you, if only to be gauging a distance before you. I am here, but then who am I? And, rather than prompt a fixed definition, the moment invites movement, a surging advance into attention that calls on the instant for re-definition, a fleeting glance to the measure of extended breathing.

For a long time, this has been the case. Descartes once made a reasonable proposal that caught on. His *cogito* posed the idea that thinking makes me what I am. Later that took a drastic turn when the Romantics invoked feeling. The re-consideration was all-encompassing, overwhelming, an exponential explosion. Witness the French Revolution. At the time, William Blake poised the turbulence of the phenomenon between the poles of Reason and Energy. And William Blake is where George Quasha started.

Further to resolve each disturbance into what had been long held to be an evolving process, the focus ever since has stayed on consciousness, bringing it to light as suitably individual yet varyingly kaleidoscopic. And the means engaged to achieve this, in the arts at least, dwells in renewed elaboration, customized collaboration, each a specific renegotiation at the taproot that aims to sidestep and avert approximation.

In undertaking the immense task, Quasha has come up with an achievement in proportion and scale equal to his venture. As I consider it, I can also reflect: one size does fit all, a subatomic nucleus as intricately configured as the cosmos.

The theme for today is the dailiness of all coincidence. Poetry Is. George Quasha.

Axial Drawing, Dakini Series (7 acrylic paints, 4 brushes, two-handed), 2013

Axial Drawing (graphite & color pencil, two-handed), 2008

Selected Bibliography

OF GEORGE QUASHA'S WORKS

POETRY

Books

Five Blind Men. Co-authors: Jim Harrison, Charles Simic, J.D. Reed, Dan Gerber. Fremont, MI: Sumac Press, 1969.

Amanita's Hymnal. New York: 1970; currently online.

Magic Spell for the Far Journey. New York: 1971.

Somapoetics (Book One). Fremont, MI: Sumac Press, 1973.

Word-Yum. New York: Metapoetics Press, 1974.

Giving the Lily Back Her Hands. Barrytown, NY: Station Hill Press, 1979.

Ainu Dreams. Co-author: Chie Hasegawa. Barrytown, NY: Station Hill Press: 1999.

Verbal Paradise (preverbs). Tenerife, Canary Islands: Zasterle Press: 2011.

Glossodelia Attract (preverbs). Barrytown, NY: Station Hill Press, 2015.

Things Done for Themselves (preverbs). New York: Marsh Hawk Press, 2015.

The Daimon of the Moment (preverbs). Northfield, MA: Talisman House Press, 2015.

Not Even Rabbits Go Down This Hole (preverbs). New York: Spuyten Duyvil, 2020.

Black Scintillation. Catskill, NY: Lunar Chandelier Collective Press, 2021.

Waking from Myself (preverbs). Barrytown, NY: Station Hill Press, 2021.

Chapbooks

Scorned Beauty Comes Up From Behind (preverbs). Barrytown, NY: Between Editions: 2012.

Speaking Animate (preverbs). Barrytown, NY: Between Editions: 2014.

Free Floating Instant Nations (preverbs). Annandale-on-Hudson, NY: Metambesen: www.metambesen.org, 2014.

The Eros of Soft Exterior Shocks (preverbs). Annandale-on-Hudson, NY:

Metambesen: www.metambesen
.org, 2015.

Polypoikilos: Matrix in Variance (preverbs). Dispatches from the Poetry Wars: www.dispatchespoetrywars.com, 2017.

With Ashley Garrett

Co-Configurative Eternities (preverbs for paintings by Ashley Garrett). Annandale-on-Hudson, NY: Metambesen: www.metambesen.org, 2019.

With Susan Quasha

Dowsing Axis (preverbs). www.dispatchespoetrywars.com, 2019.

Hearing Other (preverbs). www.dispatchespoetrywars.com, 2019.

Genius Foci (preverbs). www.talismanmag.net/quasha.html, 2020.

Hilaritas Sublime (preverbs). www.metambesen.org, 2020.

Surface Retention (preverbs). www.metambesen.org, 2020.

View of the Sleeping Dragon (preverbs). Blazing Stadium: blazingstadium.com, #3, 2020.

Poetry Audio and Video Recordings Online:

writing.upenn.edu/PennSound/x/Quasha.php

vimeo.com/user1534756

www.youtube.com/user/gquasha43

PROSE

On Poetry and Poetics

Poetry in Principle: Essays in Poetics. Foreword Edward S. Casey. New York: Dispatches/Spuyten Duyvil, 2019.

Writing on Art (books)

An Art of Limina: Gary Hill's Works and Writings. Co-author: Charles Stein. Foreword Lynne Cooke. Barcelona: Polígrafa, 2009.

Gary Hill: Language Willing. Barrytown, NY: further/art and Boise Art Museum, 2002.

HanD HearD/liminal objects: Gary Hill's Projective Installations, Number 1. Co-author: Charles Stein. Barrytown, NY: Station Hill Press, 1997.

Tall Ships: Gary Hill's Projective Installations, Number 2. Co-author: Charles Stein. Barrytown, NY: Station Hill Press, 1997.

Viewer: Gary Hill's Projective Installations, Number 3. Co-author: Charles Stein. Barrytown, NY: Station Hill Press: 1997.

Writing on His Own Art (books)

art is (Speaking Portraits). New York: PAJ Publications, Performance Ideas, 2016.

Axial Stones: An Art of Precarious Balance. Foreword Carter Ratcliff. Berkeley: North Atlantic Books, 2006.

Edited Anthologies

Open Poetry: Four Anthologies of Expanded Poems. Co-Editors: Ronald Gross with Emmett Williams, John Robert Colombo, Walter Lowenfels. New York: Simon & Schuster, 1973.

America a Prophecy: A New Reading of American Poetry from Pre-Columbian Times to the Present. Co-Editor: Jerome Rothenberg. New York: Random House, 1973.

An Active Anthology. Co-Editor: Susan Quasha. Fremont, MI: Sumac Press, 1974.

The Station Hill Blanchot Reader: Fiction & Literary Essays. Co-Editor: Charles Stein. Barrytown, NY: Station Hill Press, 1999.

Selected Performance Art

Mysterious Object (Performance #1) (Center for Performing Arts in Rhinebeck, August 7, 1991). Performance by Gary Hill, George Quasha, Susan Quasha, Chie Hasegawa & Charles Stein. garyhill.com.

The Madness of the Day (Oxford Museum of Modern Art in the Oxford University "medical theater," 1993). Performance by Gary Hill, George Quasha, Charles Stein & and Marine Hugonnier. garyhill.com.

Site Cite (Long Beach Museum of Art, December 3, 1993). Performance by Gary Hill, George Quasha, Charles Stein & Joan Jonas. garyhill.com.

Two Ways at Once/Deux Sens à la Fois (Musée d'art contemporain de Montréal, 1998). Performance by Gary Hill, George Quasha & Charles Stein. garyhill.com.

Spring from Undertime (Awaking Awaiting) (On the Boards, Seattle, March 3–4, 2000). Performance by Gary Hill, George Quasha & Charles Stein with collaboration by Kathy Bourbonais, Anastasia Hill, James Kessler, Torben Ulrich, and Nazneen Kateli D'Souza. garyhill.com.

On the Line (10th Biennial of Moving Images, Centre for Contemporary Art, Saint-Gervais Genève, Switzerland, November 10, 2003). Performance by Gary Hill & George Quasha. Garyhill.com.

Mind on the Line (WRO Art Center, The Ossolinski National Institute, Wroclaw, Poland, December 4, 2004; Theatre 77, Lodz, Poland, December 5, 2004; U Jezuitów Gallery, Poznan, Poland, December 7, 2004; Skolska28, Prague, Czech Republic, December 10, 2004). Performance by Gary Hill, George Quasha & Charles Stein in collaboration with Dorota Czerner and Aaron Miller. garyhill.com.

Glossodelic Attractors (Henry Art Gallery, Seattle, 2004). Performance of "Glossodelia" by Gary Hill & George Quasha. henryart.org.

Axial Video Art Works

Pulp Friction, Axial Objects, Verbal Objects, Axial Landscapes. Vimeo.com.

art is/poetry is/music is (Speaking Portraits): art-is-international.org

Selected Art Exhibitions

The Snite Museum of Art University (Notre Dame University, 2002): *art is/poetry is/music is (Speaking Portraits).*

Baumgartner Gallery, New York (Chelsea), 2004, 2005: Axial Stones & Drawings.

White Box, New York (Chelsea), 2006: *art is/poetry is/music is (Speaking Portraits).*

The Samuel Dorsky Museum (SUNY New Paltz, June 23–October 7, 2007, Sara Bedrick Gallery): *art is* and Axial works in stone, graphite, and video.

Lightforms Art Center (Hudson, NY, *April 9th, 2021–July 3rd, 2021).* Moving Forms/Dynamic Balance: Axial Stones & Drawings.

List of Illustrations

Acknowledgements

Heartfelt gratitude to the editors of these journals, presses and other publications in which some materials in this book first appeared (sometimes in earlier forms):

> AC Books; Between Editions; Dispatches Editions; Ediciones Polígrafa; further/art & Boise Art Museum; *Jacket2*; Lunar Chandelier Collective Press; Marsh Hawk Press; Metambesen Press; Metapoetics Press; North Atlantic Books; Spuyten Duyvil Publishing; Station Hill Press; Sumac Press; Talisman House, Publishers; *Talisman: A Journal of Contemporary Poetry and Poetics*; Unique Artists' Books; and Zasterle Press.

Special thanks to the Anthology Film Archives, New York City, which in 2015 held a screening of *poetry is (Speaking Portraits)* with panel discussions including a number of poets; and to Kimberly Lyons and Vyt Bakaitis who created the event.

A very special thanks to Edward Foster, the founder and Editor-in-Chief of Daniels, Jensen, Publishers / Talisman House, Publishers, as well as *Talisman: A Journal of Contemporary Poetry and Poetics* where (in Issue #45) some of the critical writings in this present book appeared in earlier versions.

Finally, I offer my especial thanks to Jerome McGann for composing the Foreword to this volume, as well to this book's assembled contributors for their deeply informed, graceful, and often brilliant critical appreciations, written in the service of illuminating George Quasha's singular achievement in our arts and ideas. These critics, poets and the like are, to my mind, without parallel, and it has been a great pleasure and honor to have shepherded their work contained herein.

B.K.

About the Authors

Vyt Bakaitis, with three books of poems published, and *Refuge & Occasion* due from Station Hill Press in early 2022, has also completed *The Antigone Play*, adapted from Sophocles by way of Hölderlin's renowned German version, and is currently editing *Transcience: or, Exile Tours*, his assorted readings in lyric poetry from various cultures. A native of Lithuania, he has been living in New York City since 1968. Recent poems have appeared in *Vanitas*, *The Brooklyn Rail*, *Talisman* and the online journal, *Eoagh*.

William Benton received his early training in music and worked as a jazz piano player before becoming a writer. His poetry has appeared in *The New Yorker*, *The Paris Review*, and other magazines. He is the author of several books of poetry, including *Birds*, *Marmalade*, and *Backlit*, as well as *Exchanging Hats*, a book on the paintings of Elizabeth Bishop, *The Mary Julia Paintings of Joan Brown*, and *Madly*, a novel. His most recent books are a reissue of *Birds*, from Nightboat Books and *Reliquaries, The Sculpture of Ted Waltz*. A new edition of *Marmalade* is forthcoming from Station Hill Press. He lives in New York City.

Edward Casey is Distinguished Professor at SUNY, Stony Brook. He has written a number of books of a phenomenological bent: among them *Imagining; Remembering; Getting Back into Place;* and *The Fate of Place*. In *Spirit and Soul*, he traces out archetypal dimensions of imagination, memory, and place. More recently, he has pursued what he has dubbed as "periphenomenology" in such books as *The World at a Glance*, *The World on Edge*, and *Turning Emotion Inside Out*. In the last-named book, the influence of George Quasha's notion of "ecoproprioception" is evident. A former president of the American Philosophical Association (Eastern Division), he has created a master's program located at the Brooklyn Commons whose title is "Philosophy and the Arts" and in which George Quasha has been a frequent and welcome guest.

Thomas Fink has published 11 books of poetry—most recently *A Pageant for Every Addiction* (Marsh Hawk Press, 2020), written collaboratively with Maya D. Mason, *Hedge Fund Certainty* (Meritage Press and i.e. Press, 2019) and *Selected Poems & Poetic Series* (Marsh Hawk Press, 2016). His books of criticism include *"A Different Sense of Power": Problems of Community in Late Twentieth-Century U.S. Poetry* (Fairleigh Dickinson University Press, 2001) and the co-edited anthology, *Reading the Difficulties: Dialogues with Contemporary American Innovative Poetry* (University of Alabama Press, 2014). His work appeared in *Best American Poetry 2007*, edited by David Lehman and Heather McHugh. His paintings hang in various collections. Fink is Professor of English at CUNY-LaGuardia.

Christopher Funkhouser is a writer, musician, and multimedia artist. He is author of two scholarly monographs, *Prehistoric Digital Poetry: An Archeology of Forms, 1959-1995* and *New Directions in Digital Poetry*. His poetry chapbooks include the titles *pressAgain*, *Subsoil Lutes*, and *Electro Þerdix*. In 2009, he was commissioned by the Associated Press to prepare digital poems for the occasion of Barack Obama's inauguration. In 2016, he performed at the Whitney Museum's "Open Plan: Cecil Taylor" exhibition. Funkhouser teaches at New Jersey Institute of Technology, is a Contributing Editor at *PennSound,* and hosts "POET RAY'D YO" on WGXC in Hudson, NY.

Matt Hill is a sculptor, poet, and fiction writer residing in the southern part of Northern California. His poetry, prose, fiction and reviews can be found in print and on many Internet venues, including BlazeVox Books, Gradient Books, Moira Press, Big Bridge, Chiron Review, Rain Taxi Review and Talisman. *Yet Another Blunted Ascent* and *Tertium Quid* are his latest books (Moira Press, 2017).

Andrew Joron is the author of *The Absolute Letter*, a collection of poems published by Flood Editions (2017). Joron's previous poetry collections include *Trance Archive: New and Selected Poems* (City Lights, 2010), *The*

Removes (Hard Press, 1999), *Fathom* (Black Square Editions, 2003), and *The Sound Mirror* (Flood Editions, 2008). *The Cry at Zero*, a selection of his prose poems and critical essays, was published by Counterpath Press in 2007. From the German, he has translated the *Literary Essays* of Marxist-Utopian philosopher Ernst Bloch (Stanford University Press, 1998) and *The Perpetual Motion Machine* by the proto-Dada fantasist Paul Scheerbart (Wakefield Press, 2011). As a musician, Joron plays the theremin in various experimental and free-jazz ensembles. Joron teaches creative writing at San Francisco State University.

Robert Kelly teaches in the Written Arts Program at Bard College in Annandale, where he lives with his wife, the translator Charlotte Mandell. He's written many books of poetry, some of fiction, and a few of essays and drama. Coming out this fall are a long poem, *The Cup,* a gathering of his fairy tales called *Shadow Talk,* and a big *Collected Stories*—all from McPherson & Co. Recently published companion volumes from Contra Mundum Press are *A Voice Full of Cities: The Collected Essays of Robert Kelly* (2014), ed. Pierre Joris, Peter Cockelbergh, et al. and *A City Full of Voices: Essays on the Work of Robert Kelly* (2020), a huge gathering of essays about his work by many writers and scholars, ed. Pierre Joris.

Burt Kimmelman is a distinguished professor of Humanities at New Jersey Institute of Technology. He has published ten collections of poems as well as nine volumes of criticism (including three monographs, one of them the first full-length study of the work of William Bronk), and well over a hundred articles mostly on literature, some on art, architecture, and culture. His latest book is *Visible at Dusk: Selected Essays* (Dos Madres Press, 2021). His eleventh collection of poems, *Steeple at Sunrise: New Poems* (Marsh Hawk Press, 2022), is forthcoming in 2022.

Kimberly Lyons' books of poetry include *Capella* (Oread Press, 2018), *Approximately Near* (Metambesen.org, 2016), *Soonest Mended* (Belladonna Collaborative, 2015), *Calcinatio* (Faux Press, 2014, and a limited edition collaboration with artist Ed Epping, *Mettle* (Granary Books, 1996). Work has appeared in Blazing Stadium, Local Knowledge, Unarmed, Live Mag, Middlemarch, New American Writing, and Boog Lit, among other magazines. Her essays on the poetry of Joe Ceravolo and on the paintings and drawings of Basil King have appeared in the journals *Paper 2, Talisman* and *Dispatches from the Poetry Wars*. She has an essay in *Message Ahead: Poets Respond to the Poems of Jonas Mekas* (Brooklyn Rail Editions, 2019) and an essay on poet Mina Loy's novel, *Insel*, is included in the anthology of essays, *A Forest of Many Stems* (Nightboat, 2021).

Jerome McGann is Emeritus University Professor, University of Virginia, and Visiting Research Professor, University of California, Berkeley. His most recent scholarly works are in press, *Byron Language Poetics* (Cambridge University Press) and *Language and Culture at Crossed Purposes. The Unsettled Documents of American Settlement* (University of Chicago Press). He is currently working on an online editorial project to present the literary and scholarly works of Jaime de Angulo, starting with de Angulo's ethnopoetic masterpiece *Old Time Stories* (aka *Indian Tales*). He has published six books of poetry, most recently the nonsense parodies *Children's Ours* (2020), and prepared poetic stage adaptations of various "unplayable" Romantic works, including Byron's *Manfred* and *Cain*, Beddoes' *Death's Jest Book*, and a dramatic version of Blake's *The Marriage of Heaven and Hell.* Station Hill will shortly reissue his 1998 *Poetics of Sensibility. A Revolution in Literary Style.*

Cheryl Pallant is the author of twelve books, most recently the poetry collection *Her Body Listening* (Blaze Vox Books, 2017), and the nonfiction book *Writing and the Body in Motion: Awakening Voice through Somatic Practice* (McFarland and Company. 2018). Station Hill Press published her first two poetry collections, *Uncommon Grammar Cloth* (2001) and *Into Stillness* (2003). Poetry, fiction, and nonfiction have appeared in numerous print and online magazines such as *Empty Mirror, Fence Magazine, Oxford Magazine,* and *Café Irreal*, and in several anthologies. She has a PhD in somatic writing and teaches writing and dance at University of Richmond, leads Writing From the Body workshops internationally, and is a Reiki and Healing Touch practitioner.

Tamas Panitz is the author of several poetry books, including *Toad's Sanctuary* (Ornithopter Press, 2021) and *The House of the Devil* (Lunar Chandelier Collective, 2020). He is a founding editor of the online journal *Blazing Stadium*. Tamas Panitz is also a painter, whose paintings and stray poems can be found on Instagram, @tamaspanitz.

Carter Ratcliff is a poet and art critic. Among his books of poetry are *Fever Coast* (1973), *Give Me Tomorrow* (1983), and *Arivederci, Modernismo* (2007). He is the author of *The Fate of a Gesture: Jackson Pollock and Postwar American Art* (1996) and has written monographs on Lee Krasner, Alex Katz, Andy Warhol, and John Singer Sargent, among others. His essays on art have appeared in leading journals, American and European. He is an adviser to the Pollock-Krasner Foundation. His first novel, *Tequila Mockingbird* was published by Station Hill Press in 2015.

Gary Shapiro is Tucker-Boatwright Professor of Philosophy and Humanities Emeritus at the University of Richmond. He holds BA and PhD degrees from Columbia University. Shapiro's five single-authored books are: *Nietzschean Narratives* (1989); *Alcyone: Nietzsche on Gifts, Noise, and Women* (1991); *Earthwards: Robert Smithson and Art After Babel* (1995); *Archaeologies of Vision: Foucault and Nietzsche on Seeing and Saying* (2003); *Nietzsche's Earth: Great Events, Great Politics* (2016). Shapiro has published many articles in aesthetics, continental philosophy, and various aspects of the history of philosophy. In recent years he has published essays exploring intersections of literature and philosophy; these include articles focusing on Herman Melville, J.M. Coetzee, Nietzsche's reception of Dostoevsky, and Richard Powers' *The Overstory*. Shapiro is currently working on two books: a philosophical study of F. Scott Fitzgerald and a memoir articulating the history and culture of American crime families with Frankfurt School racket theory.

Charles Stein's work comprises a complexly integrated field of poems, prose reflections, translations, drawings, photographs, lectures, conversations, and performances. Born in 1944 in New York City, he is the author of many books of poetry including *The Hat Rack Tree* (Station Hill Press, 1994), *Black Light Casts White Shadows* (Lunar Chandelier, 2018), *There Where You Do Not Think to be Thinking* (Spuyten Duyvil, 2015), *From Mimir's Head* (Station Hill Press, 2011), a verse translation of *The Odyssey* (North Atlantic Books, 2008), and a forthcoming translation of *The Iliad* (Station Hill Press). His prose writings include a vision of the Eleusinian Mysteries, *Persephone Unveiled* (North Atlantic Books, 2006), a critical study of poet Charles Olson's use of the writing of C.G. Jung, *The Secret of the Black Chrysanthemum* (Station Hill Press, 1987), and a collaborative study with George Quasha of the work of Gary Hill, *An Art of Limina: Gary Hill's Works & Writings* (Ediciones Polígrafa, 2009). His facsimile collection of ink pictures, *Twelve Drawings,* was published by Station Hill in 2018. He holds a PhD in literature from the University of Connecticut at Storrs and lives with guitarist, choral director, and research historian, Megan Hastie in Barrytown, New York.

George Quasha, 2018